A Mechanical Account Of Poisons In Several Essays

Mead, Richard, 1673-1754

A

Mechanical Account

OF

POISONS

In Several

ESSAYS.

A

Mechanical Account

OF

POISONS

In Several

ESSAYS.

BY

RICHARD MEAD, M.D.F.R.S.
And Phyſician to St. *Thomas*'s Hoſpital.

The Second Edition, Reviſed, with Additions.

LONDON:

Printed by *J. M.* for Ralph Smith, at
the *Bible*, under the *Piazza's*, of the
Royal Exchange, Cornhill. 1708.

THE
PREFACE.

TO give an exact and particular Account of the Nature and Manner of acting of Poisons, *is no easie Matter ; but to Discourse more intelligibly of* Them *than Authors have hitherto done, not very difficult. One may without much Pains shew their Effects to be owing to something more than the bare Qualities of Heat or Cold ; and Discover the Footsteps of* Mechanism *in those surprizing* Phænomena *which are commonly ascribed to some* Occult *or* Unknown Principle. *But to Unravel the Springs of the several Motions upon which such* Appearances

A 3   *do*

The Preface.

do depend, and *Trace* up all the *Symp-toms* to their *Firſt Cauſes*, requires ſome *Art* as well as *Labour* ; and that both upon the account of the *Exquiſite Fineneſs*, and *marvellous Compoſition*, of the *Animal Machine* in which they are *Tranſacted*, and of the *Minute-neſs* of thoſe *Bodies* which have the force to induce in it ſuch *Sudden* and *Violent Alterations*.

I have attempted ſomewhat this way in the following *Eſſays* ; in which *I* do not promiſe *Methodical*, and *Fi-niſh'd Treatiſes*, but only ſome ſhort *Hints* of *Natural Hiſtory*, and *Rude Strokes* of *Reaſoning* ; which, if put together, and rightly *Improved*, may perhaps ſerve to furniſh out a more to-lerable SPECIMEN of the DOC-TRINE of POISONS, than has yet been *Publiſhed*.

The

The Preface.

The First Draught of this small Piece, I made some Years since, Entertaining my self at Leisure Hours, with Experiments on Vipers, and other Venomous Creatures ; Examining now and then the Texture of Arsenic, Mercury Sublimate, and the like Malignant Substances ; Turning over what Authors had said on the several Subjects, and making such Remarks as from Time to Time Occurr'd.

These continued Enquiries made up at last, Three or Four short Discourses ; which, when I began to Digest into Order, the Increase of Business contracted the Intervals of my spare Time ; and the Diversion of such Studies quickly giving way to the Severity of more Necessary Labours, They were quite thrown by. Till Talking not long since with Dr. Areskine, concerning the Viper,

I took

The Preface.

I took Occasion to review my scattered Papers, and confirm my Reasonings by New Experiments. He very readily offered *Me* His *Anatomical Observations;* These I have put at the End of the First Essay; Which do no not promise a *Complete Dissection of the Animal,* but chiefly shew the Make of those *Parts* which are concern'd in the Poison.

My Design, in Thinking of These Matters, was, to Try how far I could carry Mechanical Considerations *in Accounting for those Surprizing Changes,* which Poisons *make in an Animal Body;* Concluding (as I think, fairly) that if so abstruse Phænomena *as* These did come *under the known Laws of* Motion, It might very well be taken for granted, that the more obvious Appearances in the same Fabrick are owing to such Causes as are within the Reach of Geometrical Reasoning;

The Preface.

soning; And that therefore as the first Step towards the Removal of a Disease is to know Its Origin, so he is likely to be the best Physician, who having the same assistance of Observations and Histories with Others, does best understand the Humane *Oeconomy, the Texture of the Parts, Motions of the Fluids, and the Power which other Bodies have to make Alterations in any of These.*

Nor indeed ought any One to Doubt of This, who considers that the Animal Compages *is not an irregular Mass, and disorderly Jumble of Atoms, but the Contrivance of Infinite Wisdom, and Master-piece of that Creating Power, who has been pleased to do all Things by Establish'd Laws and Rules, and that Harmony and Proportion should be the Beauty of all his Works.*

The Preface.

It were therefore heartily to be wish'd, that those Gentlemen who are so much afraid of Introducing Mathematical *Studies, that is,* Demonstration and Truth, *into the Practice of* Physick, *were so far at least Instructed in the necessary Disciplines, as to be able to pass a true Judgment, what Progress and Advances may be made this way; They would not then perhaps Decry an Attempt of so much Moment to the Wellfare of Mankind, as vain and impossible, because it is difficult, and requires Application and Pains.*

It is very evident, that all other Methods of Improving Medicine have been found Ineffectual, by the Stand it has been at these two or three Thousand Years ; and that since of late Mathematicians *have set Themselves to the Study of it, Men do already begin to Talk so Intelligibly and Comprehensibly, even about abstruse Matters, that it*

maʃ

The Preface.

may be hop'd in a short time, if Those who are Design'd for this Profession, are early, while their Minds and Bodies are Patient of Labour and Toil, Initiated in the Knowledge of Numbers and Geometry, that Mathematical Learning will be the Distinguishing Mark of a Physician from a Quack; and that He who wants this necessary Qualification, will be as Ridiculous as one without Greek or Latin.

I have, as to what regards the Animal Oeconomy, Referr'd as much as I could to the Works of Bellini, which have brought great Light into the Dark Regions of Physick, and Taught Us to argue clearly and consistently, instead of Amusing our selves with Unintelligible Words or Precarious Hypotheses. The Dissertations of Dr. Pitcarne, who is the Honour of his Profession in Scotland, are a Convincing Proof of the Advantage of such a
Mechanical

The Preface.

Mechanical Way of Reasoning ; nor could Malice *it self deny This, were not* Ignorance *in Confederacy with it, which will secure any One from being Benefitted by the most useful Demonstrations.*

Notwithstanding This, I have been forced now and then to make Digressions from my Subject, to clear some Doctrines necessary to be known which have not been Explained by others. For indeed the Data from which We argue in these Matters are by many too few. Dr. Cheyne, *the Author of the* New Theory of Fevers, *has enumerated several Particulars in which the* Theoretic Part of Medicine *still wants Improvement. If these Deficiencies were made good, We might with more Ease Proceed in our Enquiries into Human Nature, and should soon Convince the World, that the most useful of Arts, if duly Cultivated, is more than meer* Conjecture, *or base* Empiricism.   *As*

The Preface.

As to the Authors I have made use of, who have Treated of Poisons, *I have Quoted only those who Furnished me with Matter of Fact ; For there are but few* Originals ; *and very large Volumes on this Subject do many times contain little more than a Collection of* Vulgar Errors.

I had once Thought to have carried these Searches *farther ; in Particular, besides what is occasionally mention'd in the last Essay concerning Infection in acute Diseases, to have enquired into the Nature of* Contagious *and* Hereditary Distempers. *But the Humour of Scribling would not hold out ; And some perhaps will say, 'Tis well enough it didn't ; For I am not Ignorant how Few I am like to Please ; If it be hard to Think and Write Justly, 'tis harder yet to Bring Others to one's own Taste ; Nor shall I be at all Angry, if to Many I have afforded Matter of Satyr and Invective ;*

The Preface.

Invective; *Less Wit suffices for These than for the Discovery of Useful Truths. They who have no Smattering of Mathematical Knowledge, are incompetent Judges of what Service I have done towards the Improvement of the Theory, or* Practice *of* Medicine, *and Those who are acquainted with these* Matters, *will, it may be, think it something to* Talk *Intelligibly on such difficult and abstruse* Points. *I neither want* Applause, *nor fear* Censure; *and therefore be the Fate of These Papers what it will, as they were first Penn'd for my own* Satisfaction, *and* Innocent Entertainment; *so I am resolved They shall never Ingage me in the Trouble of* Quarrels *or* Disputes.

T H E

THE
CONTENTS.

ESSAY

E S S A Y. I.

O F T H E

V I P E R.

THE Viper has always been ſo Notorious for its Venom, that the moſt remote Antiquity made it an Emblem of what is Hurtful and Deſtructive. Nay, ſo terrible was the Nature of theſe Creatures, that they were very commonly thought to be ſent as Executioners of Divine Vengeance upon Mankind for E-normous Crimes, which had eſcaped the Courſe of Common Juſtice. Thus *Hero-dotus (a)* and *Ælian (b)* do both take no-tice that Adders were ſacred among the *Ægyptians* ; that they affirmed of one ſort

(a). *Lib.* 2. *Cap.* 74. (b) *De Animalib. lib.* 17. *c.* 5.

B of

of 'em particularly, that they were made to be Minifters of the Will of the Gods, by averting Evil from Good Men, and punifhing the Bad. And *Paufanias* (*c*) obferves of the *Arabians*, that they forbore to offer any Violence to the Vipers which were found near to the Balfam-Tree, as reputing 'em Holy. The Footfteps of which Superftition do ftill remain among thefe People to this very Day, for *Veflingius* (*d*) faw many of 'em take thefe Creatures into their Houfes, feed 'em, and worfhip them as the *Genii* of the Place. The fame odd Fancy obtains in the *Eaft-Indies*, for the King of *Calicut* caufes Cottages to be fet up for Serpents to keep them from the Rain, and makes it Death to any that fhall hurt one of 'em ; thinking them to be Heavenly Spirits, becaufe they can fo fuddenly Kill Men (*e*). A Remarkable Inftance of fuch an Opinion as this we have in the Hiftory of St. *Paul* (*f*), whom the People of *Malta* when they faw the Viper leap upon his Hand, prefently concluded to be a Murderer, and as readily made a

---

(c) *Bœotic.* p. m. 303.
(d) *Not. in Alpin. de Plant. Ægypt.* Cap. 14.
(e) *Purchafe's* Pilgrimage, *l.* 5. *c.* 12.
(f) Act. Apoft. *Chap.* 28.

God

God of him, when inftead of having his Hand Inflamed, or falling down Dead, (one or other of which is ufually the Effect of thofe Bites) he without any harm fhook the Beaft into the Fire. It being Obvious enough to imagine, that He muft ftand in a near Relation at leaft to the Gods themfelves, who could thus Command the Meffengers of their Vengeance, and Counterwork the Effects of fuch powerful Agents.

And this, after the many Conjectures upon the Matter, feems to be the true Reafon why Antiquity not only Reprefented the Firft Mafters of Phyfick, *Hermes, Æfculapius, Hippocrates,* &c. in their Statues and Medals, with a Viper added to their Figure, but alfo Worfhipped them under this Form; for Difeafes in thofe Days, efpecially the moft Violent, Plagues, Fevers, &c. were in like manner, as thefe Creatures, reputed the Commiffion'd Meffengers of Divine Anger and Difpleafure (g). They therefore who by their Art could Cure and Stop the Courfe of thefe, as they were fuppofed to do this by the particular Leave

(g) *Leg. Cornel. Celf. præfat. in Medicin. Morbos ait vetuftiffimis temporib. ad Iram Deorum immortalium relatos effe, & ab iifdem opem pofci folitam.*

and

and Affiftance of Heaven, fo had Ho-
nours paid to Them accordingly, and this
Reprefentation was in the Nature of an
Hieroglyphick Character ; for as the
Learned *Spanhem* obferves, *(h)* the Viper
was a Symbol or Emblem of Divine Power.

Macrobius indeed gives us another account of this Cuftom, and that is from the
Property which all Serpents have of caft-
ing their *Exuviæ,* or Upper-Skin, every
Year, which makes 'em fit Emblems or
Reprefentations of Health ; the Recovery
of which from Sicknefs and Difeafes may
juftly be looked upon as the beginning of
a frefh Period of Life, and (as the
throwing off the *Senectus* of thefe Creatures feems to be) the Renewing of
Age *(i).*

Whether one or the other of thefe
Reafons be allow'd of, or both thought
good, certain it is that fuch fond and fu-
perftitious Fancies concerning the Viper,
together with the miftaken Opinion that
few of its Parts were exempt from Poi-

(h) *Divinæ Potentiæ Symbolum. Vid. Exec. Spanhem. De*
    Ufu Numifmat. p. m. 125, 126, & 181, & feq;
(i) *Saturnal. Lib. 1. c. 20. Ideo Simulachris Eorum (Æfcu-*
    lapii & Salutis) junguntur figuræ Draconum quia præftant
    ut humana Corpora velut infirmitatis pelle depofitâ, ad
    priftinum revirefcant vigorem, ut virefcunt Dracones per
    annos fingulos pelle fenectutis exutâ.

fon, did not fuffer the Ancients to make
any Curious Enquiries into its Nature by
Anatomy and Experiments, and this is
the Caufe of the many Errors they have
delivered down to us in thefe Points,
which by gradual Advances have fince
been rectified, and the inward Make, Properties, and Generation of this Animal,
largely treated of; more efpecially M.
Redi (k), *Charas* (l), and Dr. *Tyfon* in
his Diffection of the *Rattle-Snake* (m),
which is a larger Species of a Viper, have
taken Pains on this Subject, to whofe Dif-
coveries, what is yet wanting, we fhall
add at the End of this Effay.

The Symptoms which follow upon
the Bite of a Viper, when it faftens either
one or both its greater Teeth in any Part
of the Body, are an acute Pain in the
Place Wounded, with a Swelling at firft
Red, but afterwards Livid, which by
degrees fpreads farther to the Neighbouring Parts with great Faintnefs, and a
Quick, tho' Low, and fometimes Interrupted Pulfe, great Sicknefs at the Stomach,
with Bilious, Convulfive Vomitings, Cold
Sweats, and fometimes Pains about the

(k) *Offervazioni intorno alle Vipere.*
(l) *Nouvelles Experiences fur la Vipere.*
(m) Philofophical Tranfactions, *Vol. XII. No.* 144.

Navel,

Navel ; and if the Cure be not fpeedy,
Death it felf, unlefs the Strength of Nature prove fufficient to overcome thefe
Diforders ; and tho' it does, the Swelling
ftill continues inflamed for fome time ;
nay, in fome Cafes more confiderably upon the abating of the other Symptoms,
than at the beginning ; and often from
the fmall Wound runs a fanious Liquor,
and little Puftules are raifed about it ; the
colour of the whole Skin is changed Yellow, as if the Patient had the *Jaundice*.

Thefe Mifchiefs, altho' different Climates, Seafon of the Year more or lefs
Hot, the greater or leffer Rage of the Viper, the Beaft it felf of a larger or fmaller
Size, and confequently able to communicate more or lefs Venom, and the like
Circumftances, may varioufly heighten or
abate 'em, yet do ufually difcover themfelves much after the fame manner in all ;
unlefs the Bite happen not to be accompanied with the Effufion of that *Liquor*,
which is the main Inftrument and Caufe
of this violent and fhocking Difturbance.

But before I proceed to enquire into
the Nature and Manner of Acting of this
Juice, it may be worth the while to take
Notice, that this is not made on purpofe
to be deadly and deftructive to *Mankind* ;
but

but that the true Defign of it is (tho' Authors have not regarded it) to perform an Office and Service of fo great Moment, to the Prefervation of the Individual, that without it this Creature could not fubfift.

For Vipers live chiefly upon Lizzards, Frogs, Toads, Mice, Moles, and the like Animals, which they do not chew, but fwallow down whole, and they lie in the Stomach; or if that be not big enough to receive them, partly in that, and partly in the OEfophagus, which is membranous and capable of great Diftenfion, till by the Salival Juices of thofe Parts, together with the Help of the Fibres of the Stomach, and the Contraction of the Mufcles of the Abdomen, they are gradually diffolved into a Fluid Subftance, fit for the Nourifhment of their Bodies, which is the Work of many Days; this is *one* Reafon why thefe Creatures can live fo long without taking any frefh Food, which I have known them to do Three or Four Months; as *another* is, that their Blood is a groffer and more vifcid Fluid than that of moft other Animals; fo that there is but a very little expence of it by Tranfpiration, and confequently lefs need of Recruit; this not

B 4 only

only *Microfcopes* difcover, but Reafon teaches; becaufe there is but very little Mufcular Force in the Stomach to comminute the Food, and make a Chyle of fine Parts, and therefore the Blood muft accordingly be of a Tough and Clammy Confiftence. Befides, the Heart of a Viper has properly but one Ventricle, and the Circulation of the Blood is performed after the fame Manner as it is in a Frog and Tortoife, in which not above one Third of it paffes thro' the Lungs; upon which Account its Comminution in them by the Air is proportionably leffer than in other Animals. Now fuch a manner of Feeding as *this* does neceffarily require, that the Prey fhould upon the firft Catching be immediately kill'd, otherwife it were by no means fit to be let into the Stomach; for we are not to think that the Force of this Part would be alone fufficient to deftroy it, the Subtilty of a living Creature (befides the Confideration of the Weaknefs of the Fibres) being in a great Meafure able to elude *that*, as indeed we do every Day find live Animals in the Ventricles of others; and therefore to do *this* is the proper Ufe both of the Teeth and their Poifon; for which being defigned and adapted, it is no wonder if the Viper, this fame Way by

which

which it deftroys its Prey, proves fometimes mifchievous to any other Creatures befides, when it happens to be enraged, or by any Provocation ftirr'd up to bite.

The Defcription of the Poifonous *Fangs*, their Make, Articulation and Motion, as alfo of the Glands that feparate the Yellowifh Liquor, and the Bags that contain it; I fhall give, together with fome Anatomical Obfervations, at the End of this Difcourfe.

This Venomous Juice it felf is of fo inconfiderable a quantity, that it is no more than one good *Drop* that does the Execution; and for this reafon Authors have contented themfelves with Trials of the Bite upon feveral Animals, never Effaying to examine the Texture and Make of the Liquor it felf; for which purpofe I have oftentimes by holding a Viper advantageoufly, and inraging it till it ftruck out its Teeth, made it to bite upon fomewhat folid, fo as to void its Poifon; which carefully putting upon a Glafs Plate, I have with a Microfcope, as nicely as I could, viewed its Parts and Compofition.

Upon the firft Sight I could difcover nothing but a Parcel of fmall Salts nimbly floating in the Liquor, but in a very fhort time the Appearance was changed, and

and thefe faline Particles were now fhot
out as it were into *Cryftals* of an incredi-
ble Tenuity and Sharpnefs, with fomething
like Knots here and there, from which
they feemed to proceed, fo that the
whole Texture did in a manner reprefent
a *Spider's Webb*, tho' infinitely Finer, and
more Minute; and yet withal fo rigid
were thefe pellucid *Spicula*, or *Darts*, that
they remained unaltered upon my Glafs
for feveral Months (*n*).

I have made feveral Trials with this
Juice in order to find out under what
Tribe of Salts thefe Cryftals are to be ranged; and not without fome difficulty, by
reafon of the Minute Quantity of the Liquor, and the Hazard of Experiments of
this Nature, have plainly feen that it does,
as an *Acid*, turn the blue Tincture of *He-
liotropium* to a Red Colour.

I did not fucceed fo well in mixing it
with Syrup of Violets, and yet it did really feem to induce in this a *Reddifh Hue*;
but I am very certain it did not at all
change it to a *Greenifh* Colour, as it
would have done if any ways *Alcalious*.

This may fuffice in their own way of
arguing, to convince thofe Gentlemen,

(n) *Vid. Fig.* 19.

who

who without the Affiftance of any Experiments, meerly to ferve an *Hypothefis*
which they have too fondly taken up,
have with great Affurance told the World,
that the Viperine Venom is an *Alcali*,
and confequently to be cured by *Acid*
Remedies. But it is by far more eafie to
Spin out a falfe Notion into precarious
Reafonings, than to make faithful Experiments, and fairly improve 'em by juft and
neceffary Confequences.

To proceed, this Difcovery agrees very well with a Relation communicated
by an Ingenious Perfon to Dr. *Tyfon*,
which does fo much illuftrate this Matter,
that I fhall tranfcribe it in his own Words,
out of the before cited *Philofophical
Tranfactions*; he fays then, That being
in the *Indies*, there came to him an *Indian* with feveral Sorts of *Serpents*, offering
to fhew him fome Experiments about the
Force of their Poifon; having therefore
firft pulled out a large One, the *Indian*
told him this would do no Harm; and
making a Ligature on his Arm as in let-
ting Blood, he expofed it naked to the
Serpent, being firft irritated to make him
bite it; the Blood that came out of the
Wound made by his Teeth, he gathered
with his Finger, and laid it on his
Thigh,

Thigh, till he had got near a Spoonful, after this he takes out another called *Cobra de Capelo*, which was leſſer, and inlarges much upon the Greatneſs of his Poiſon ; to ſhew an Inſtance of it, graſping it out about the Neck, he expreſſes ſome of the Liquor in the Bags of the Gums, about the Quantity of half a Grain, and this he puts to the coagulated Blood on his Thigh, which immediately put it into a great *Fermentation*, and working like *Barme*, changed it into a *Yellowiſh* Liquor.

This I ſay does well enough accord with what we have been advancing concerning the Nature of this *Juice* ; for Mr. *Boyle* has long ſince proved by Experiments, that there is nothing of Acid in human Blood ; and Dr. *Pitcarn* (o) has demonſtrated, that the *Acid Subſtances* of Vegetables taken into the Stomach, are by the Action of this Part, the Lungs and Heart, when they come into the BloodVeſſels, turn'd to *Alcalious* ; ſo that the Arterial Fluid muſt neceſſarily be conſidered as an *Alcali* ; and therefore according to the known Principles of Chymiſtry, its mixture with ſuch a Liquor as we have

(o) *Diſſertatio de Opera quam præſtant Corpora Acida vel Alcalica in Curatione Morborum.*

dif-

difcovered the Viperine *Sanies* to be, will always exhibit fome fuch appearance as this now related.

But not to engage any farther in thefe fort of Controverfies, we may perhaps from the foregoing Obfervations receive fome Light in order to underftand the Nature and Reafon of all thofe Symptoms which attend the Bite of this Creature. For the pungent Salts of this Venom, when with Force thrown into the Wound, will not only as fo many *Stimuli*, irritate and fret the fenfile Membranes, whereupon there neceffarily follows a greater Afflux than ordinary of the Animal Juices that way, (as is manifeft from the *Bellinian* Doctrine, *De Stimulis*) fo that the wounded Part muft be Swelled, Inflamed, Livid, *&c.* but alfo thefe *Spicula* being mixt with the Blood, will fo disjoin and difunite the Parts of it, that its Mixture muft be quite alter'd; and from the various *Cohæfion* of its *Globules* will arife fuch different Degrees of *Fluidity* and *Impulfe* towards the Parts, *&c.* from what this Liquor had before, that its very Nature will be changed, or in the common way of fpeaking, it will be truly and really *Fermented.*

To

To underftand aright how all this is done, it is neceffary to hint fomewhat concerning the Nature of *Fluids* in General, and thofe Alterations in them which we call *Fermentations*; for I fhall retain this known Word, tho' in the proper Senfe in which 'tis commonly ufed, there can be no *Fermenting* of the Liquors in the Animal Body.

And here I muft refer to the Treatife of *Bellini de Fermentis*, who has with great Clearnefs fhewn, that there is in all *Fluids* not only a fimple *Contact* of their Parts, but alfo a *nifus in Contactum*, or *Cohæfion*, and this of a certain *Degree* or *Force*, and befides, of a particular *Direction*; which is indeed, tho' exprefs'd in other words, the very fame thing with the *Attraction* of the Particles one to another; This Mr. *Newton* has demonftrated to be the great Principle of Action in the Univerfe, has taught us the Laws of it in the greater Quantities and Collections of *Matter*; and he who rightly Studies his Philofophy will underftand that the fame obtains in the moft Minute and Fineft Corpufcles, which do unite into Bodies of different *Solidity* and *Make*, according to the Degree with which they do mutually *attract* each other, and to the *Super-ficies,*

ficies, by which, when drawn, they do *touch* and *adhere.* To this if we add a *Preſſion* of the ſeveral Parts of the Fluid every way, and conſider withal, that this *Uniform* Attraction of the Parts to one another muſt be variouſly changed by the different Attraction of Hetero-geneous Bodies mixt with them, we have the great Principles of all Fluids, up-on which their ſeveral *Phænomena* do de-pend

And hence it follows, that whatſoever *Power* is ſufficient to make a Change in this Attraction, or Cohæſion of the Parts, makes an Alteration of the Nature of the Fluid; that is, as the Chymiſts expreſs it, puts it into a *Fermentation.* And if any one ſhall think it neceſſary to enquire in-to the particular Manner of producing ſuch an Effect, we may perhaps in ſo ab-ſtruſe a Matter not improbably Conjecture *thus,* That our Blood conſiſting chiefly of Two Parts, a ſimple *Lymph,* and an in-finite Number of ſmall *Globules,* contain-ing a very ſubtle and elaſtic Fluid, theſe acute Salts, when mingled with it, do prick thoſe Globules, or *Veſiculæ,* and ſo let out their impriſoned active Subſtance, which expanding it ſelf every way, muſt neceſſa-rily be the Inſtrument of this ſpeedy Al-teration

teration and Change *(p)*. From such an *Hypothefis* as this (and, it may be, not very eafily from any other) we may account for many of the furprizing Phænomena in the Fermentations of Liquors; and as precarious as it feems, its Simplicity, and Plainnefs, and Agreement with the fore-mentioned Doctrine, will, I believe, recommend it before any other to thofe who are not unacquainted with *Geometrical* Reafonings. But I wave thefe Confiderations at prefent, and fhall only add One Remark or Two with Relation to the purpofe in Hand, and fo proceed.

In the firft place then, we may from this *Theory,* learn, how it comes to pafs that fo fmall a Portion of Juice fhould infect fo great a quantity of Liquor; for in order to do this, it is not neceffary that the Venom fhould be at the very firft mixt with all its Parts; but it is fufficient that it prick fome of the *Bladders,* and the elaftic Matter of thefe being let out, will be a nimble *Vehicle* to the acute Salts, and not only by its activity difperfe them thro' the Fluid, but reftore to them their decreafing *Force,* and thus continue their Effects,

---

(p) *Vid. Bernoulli de Effervefcentia & Fermentatione.*

till

till a great part of the Liquor undergoes at leaſt, in ſome Degree, the like Alteration.

And this will the more eaſily happen in the preſent Caſe, becauſe the *Force* with which this Poiſon is thrown into the Blood, as appears from the Mechaniſm of the diſcharging Organs, is very great, and conſequently its Effects will be proportionably violent, or the Miſchief more large and diffuſed.

The want of this may be one Reaſon why the Experiment of firſt making a Wound in the Fleſh with any ſharp Inſtrument, and then dropping in the *Sanies*, may not always ſucceed ſo well in killing Animals, as one would from the preceeding Doctrine be ready to expect. Tho' if ſome amends be made for this Defect, by taking a greater quantity of the Juice, and carefully inſtilling it, It proves equally Fatal this way, as when immediately diſcharg'd from the Viper it ſelf. Thus it might happen that thoſe Trials of this kind, which were happily made by Sr *Redi*, might not however convince Mr *Charas*, in as much as there is oftentimes a great deal of difference in the Event of Experiments, when made with Purpoſe, and a Deſign that they ſhould ſucceed, and when

C   Timo-

Timorously and Cautiously managed, left they should unluckily overthrow a darling *Hypothesis.*

The other Observation I shall draw from the foregoing Theory, is this, That it appears from hence what a vast *variety* there may be in the Fermentations even of one and the same Fluid ; for these being no other than *Changes* made in the *Cohæsion* of the compounding Particles, are capable of as many Alterations as *Motion* in its *Degrees* and *Directions* can admit of, which are really Infinite.

This I mention with regard to some of the following *Essays,* in which, if we ascribe many Symptoms seemingly very different, to a Ferment rais'd in the Blood, it may be consider'd, that the Nature of this Cause is such, as according to the several Properties of the *Primum Agens,* or *Fermenting Power,* to bear by far more Varieties than any one can be aware of.

To return to the Viper ; the Effects of such an Agitation of the Blood, as we have been describing, must not only be whatever are the Consequences of a disturbed *Circulation,* and irregular and interrupted *Secretion* of the Spirits, as low Pulse, Faintings, Sickness, Palpitation of the Heart, Convulsive Vomitings, Tremblings

blings of the Body, &c. but alfo the *Texture* of this Fluid being thus broken, thofe
Parts of it which are of the floweft Motion, and greateft Vifcidity, will be eafily feparated from the others ; fuch they
are, which when united together do compound the *Bile*, and therefore thefe will
tinge the Capillary Veffels, and fine *Ducts*
in the Skin, with a Yellowifh Colour ;
that is, will induce an *Icterus*, or Jaundice.

For it is not only (if at all *Primarily*)
from an Obftruction of the *Biliary Canals*
that this Symptom does proceed, but alfo
from any Caufe whatfoever, which either
deftroys the Saline Part of the Bile, by
the means of which its Oil is kept mixt
with the Water of the Blood, or elfe in-
creafes the Oily and Sulphureous Part to
that Degree, that tho' it be duly impreg-
dated with Salt, yet the Watery Part of
the Blood, which can only take up a certain Proportion of it, being already *Sa-
turated*, can receive no more ; or laftly,
does, by *difuniting* the compounding Particles of the Blood, alter that *Inteftine*
Motion and Agitation which is neceffary
to carry along thro' the Veffels, together
with the more volatile Parts, thofe which
are more Clammy and Glutinous. For

in all thefe Cafes 'tis plain that the Bilious Corpufcles muft be *præcipitated* upon
thofe Parts of the Body where there is
leaft Motion, that is, upon the extreme
Superficies.

And tho' this Theory may perhaps appear extravagant, becaufe new and uncommon, yet it will not, I believe, feem
ill grounded or irrational to thofe who
underftand the Doctrine of the *Mixture*
of Heterogene Fluids, and their *Sepa-*
ration; and who withal know, that the
Veffels are rarely obftructed, unlefs it be
from the fault of the Liquid they carry,
and confequently that a Defect in the Bile
it felf muft be (excepting fome extraordinary Cafes) antecedent to the Obftruction
of the Biliary Ducts.

In fhort, the different Cure of this Difeafe confirms thefe Notions; for an *Icterus*
from the firft Caufe affign'd, which is generally owing to a fedentary Life, want of
Exercife, *&c.* and attended with an extreme Coftivenefs and white *Fæces*, is cured by Volatile, Acrimonious, and Bitter
Salts. From the Second produced oftentimes by drinking ftrong Liquors, Spirits,
&c. and accompanied with a *Diarrhœa*,
partly by Diluting and Temperating, partly by Stomachic and Strenghning Medicines.

dicines. As the laſt Species of it (for the ſake of which we have mention'd the other) is removed by ſuch *Antidotes* as overcome and deſtroy the Venomous Ferment, corrupting the Blood, and breaking its *Compages*. But to have hinted theſe things may abundantly ſuffice for the preſent.

We muſt however take Notice, That *tho'* the *main* Alterations made by this Poiſon be in the Fluid of the Arteries, *yet* that *That* of the Nerves may hereby be conſiderably *changed* too ; for *This* conſiſting, as well as the Blood of differing Parts, and being diſperſed in ſmall *Tubes* all over the Body, is not only very capable of *various* Degrees of *Force*, *Impulſe*, &c. but *Undulating* continually towards the Brain, and being the chief Inſtrument of Motion and Action, may perhaps ſometimes more immediately convey the Miſchief to the ſenſile Membranes, and thus be the Cauſe of thoſe violent Pains, Convulſions, Sickneſs, &c with which Thoſe who are Bitten are preſently ſeiz'd.

Many are the Experiments I could relate to evince the Truth of this Reaſoning concerning the Viperine Venom, which do entirely agree with thoſe made by Sʳ *Redi*, whoſe Judgment and Sincerity in Obſervations of this Nature no Body ever called in Queſtion, till Monſieur *Charas* having eſpous'd a Notion, that this Poiſon does not lie in the Yellow Liquor of the Gums, but in the enraged Spirits of the Viper, rais'd new Difficulties about the Succeſs of ſome Trials made in *France*, endeavouring thereby to invalidate the Force and Authority of thoſe made in *Italy*.

I ſhall therefore, in order to put this Matter out of all doubt, mention Two or Three Experiments made by Dr. *Areſkine*, when at *Paris*, that it may appear how defective thoſe of Mr. *Charas* are, and that the Difference of the Climate does not (as ſome began to imagine (*a*)) make any conſiderable Alteration in the Effects of this Venom, or its manner of Killing.

Firſt then, having got a large Female Viper, he made it to Bite Six Pigeons, one after another; the Firſt and Second that were bit, died within about half an Hour, one a little Time before the other; the third liv'd about two Hours; the Fourth ſeem'd to be very ſick, but reco-

---

(a) *Vid. Redi Lettera ſopra alcune oppoſitioni,* &c.

vered;

vered; the Fifth and Sixth were no more hurt than if they had been prick'd with a Pin or Needle.

Then he cut off the Head of a brisk Viper, and let it lie twenty four Hours, with the Fangs of which he wounded One Pigeon in the Breaſt, and another in the Thigh, which both expired as ſoon after, as if they had been biten by a living Viper. After this, having got a great many Vipers together, he made them bite upon a peice of Glaſs of a Cylindrical Figure, by this means preſerving the Yellow Juice which they emitted, and ſlightly wounding two Pigeons, he firſt let the Bleeding be ſtopt, then put ſome of this Liquor into the Wounds, upon which both the Pigeons died about two Hours after.

The ſame Ingenious Perſon tells me, that Monſieur *du Verney* made not only Theſe, but alſo ſeveral other Experiments of the ſame Nature, in the *Royal Acamy*, with the like Succeſs.

Theſe Proofs are ſo convincing and full, that no one, I think, can deſire more; but they will receive yet a farther Confirmation from the *Apparatus* or Mechaniſm of the Organs, with admirable Nicety contrived for the Diſcharge of this Venom, of which more by and by.

Nor is it any Objection againſt all *This*, that the *Liquor* is innocent and harmleſs in the Mouth or Stomach of any one, ſo as that it may be ſafely taſted or ſucked out of the Wound, and ſwallowed; for, *as* we obſerv'd before, that many *Acid* Subſtances taken into the Stomach are by the Action of that Part turned to *Alcalious*, ſo there is no Queſtion but theſe Saline *Spicula* are partly by the Muſcular Force of the Fibres, partly by the Salival Juice, all broken and diſſolved; or if any can paſs into the Inteſtines, the Balſam of the *Bile* will be an *Antidote* for Them; the Reaſon of which will appear when we come to the Cure.

In the mean time it may not be amiſs to Remark, That even the Ancients ſeem to have known thus much concerning the Nature of this Poiſon; of this *Galen* gives us Teſtimony in ſeverl Places; particularly in his Book *de Temperamentis* (*b*), where he takes notice, that *nothing has the ſame Power upon the human Body outwardly as inwardly; Thus* (ſays he) *neither the Venom of the Viper, nor of the Aſp, nor frothy Spittle of the Mad Dog, are alike Miſchievous when they fall upon the*

___

(b) *Lib.* 3. *Cap.* 2.

Skin,

Skin, or enter into the Stomach, as when outwardly communicated by a Wound.

The chief of the *Latin* Phyſicians (*c*), *Celſus* has elegantly expreſs'd the Matter in few Words, when adviſing to *Suck* the Wound made by the Bite ; he adds, *Neq; Hercules Scientiam præcipuam habent hi qui Pſilli nominantur, ſed audaciam uſu ipſo confirmatam, nam Venenum Serpentis, ut quædam etiam Venatoria Venena, quibus Galli præcipuè utuntur, non guſtu ſed in vulnere nocent.*

And therefore brave *Cato*, when marching the Remains of *Pompey*'s Army thro' *Africa*, very wiſely told the Soldiers, almoſt choak'd with Thirſt, yet afraid to drink of a Spring they came to, becauſe full of Serpents (*d*),

Noxia Serpentum eſt admiſto ſanguine Peſtis, Morſu Virus habent, & Fatum Dente minantur, Pocula Morte carent ————

In the like manner it was in thoſe times alſo known, that the virulent Juice had the ſame bad Effects, when mixt with the Blood, by means of a common

(*c*) *Medicin. Lib.* 5. c. 27.
(*d*) *Lucan. Pharſal.* l. 9.

Wound,

Wound, as when communicated by the Venomous Bite. This made *Celfus (e)* advife in fucking out the Poifon, to take care there be no Ulcer in the Mouth; tho' this Caution be rather flighted and ridiculed by *Severinus (f)*, and others; who do hereby difcover how little they underftood of the Seat and Nature of this Poifon. And *Galen (g)* mentioning the Story of *Cleopatra*, relates from other Authors, that fhe killed her felf *by pouring the* Virus *of an Afp into a Wound made in her Arm by her own Teeth.*

In fhort, it is upon this Foundation, that *Pliny (h)* affures us, the *Scythians* Poifon'd their Arrows with the *Sanies* of Vipers mixt with human Blood; the way of doing it *Ariftotle (i)* has at large related; and the *Tartars* are faid to ufe the like Trick to this Day. After the fame manner the *Indians* make ufe of the Venom of the Lizard, called *Gecco*; this Creature they hang up by the Tail, and by Whipping exafperate till it difcharge

---

(e) *Loc. 'ante citat.*
(f) *Vipera Pythia,* p. 361.
(g) *De Theriac. ad Pifon.* lib. 1. c. 8. *Vid. etiam* c. 10.
(h) *Nat. Hift.* lib. 11. c. 53. *Scythæ Sagittas tingunt Viperinâ Sanie & hnmano Sauguine; irremediabile id Scelus.*
(i) *De Mirabilibus.*

its *Virus*, in which they tinge their Darts ; and a very flight Wound with these Weapons is speedy Death *(k)*.

It is worth the while in the next Place to confider the Cure of this Mifchief, which without all doubt ought to be by fuch External Mannagement of the Wound as may immediately deftroy the infufed Venom.

Mr. *Boyle (l)* experienced a hot Iron held as near the Place as the Patient could poffibly endure it very effectual to this Purpofe. But the fame Method did not anfwer Expectation in the famous Cafe related by Monfieur *Charas (m)*.

An extraordinary Virtue againft this and other venomous Bites is afcribed to the *Snake-ftones* brought from the *Eaft-Indies*, one of which is to be prefently apply'd to the Part, and let ftick till it drop off ; thefe are faid to be taken out of the Head of the Serpent called by the *Portugueze, Cobra de Capelo* ; and to fuck the Poifon out of the Wound. S[r] *Redi (n)* made Trials with feveral of them, but found no Service from any.

(k) *Bontii Hiftor. Ind.* lib. 5. c. 5.
(l) Ufefulnefs of Experimental Philofophy, *Part* 2. *p.* 50.
(m) p. m. 66.
(n) *Efperienze intorno a diverfe Cofe Naturali.*

Yet

Yet *Baglivi* (*o*) tells us of a terrible Bite of a Scorpion cured this way. Monſieur *Charas* (*p*) his Pigeons all died, tho' *theſe* were immediately clapped on, and ſtuck cloſe to the Wound: But Dr. *Havers* ſaw a good Effect of *one* upon a Dog, who tho' ſeverely bitten, ſuffered no Harm, nor any farther Mark of the Poiſon than a livid Circle round the Place.

In plain Truth, *as* theſe celebrated *Stones* do not ſeem to be what it is pretended they are, but rather Factitious Bodies compounded, it may be, of Calcined Bones, and ſome Teſtaceous Matters mixt together; *ſo* by Reaſon of their ſpongy and porous Texture, they do very readily adhere to any moiſtened Part of the Fleſh, and imbibe whatſoever humidity they meet with. This their Quality any one may experience by holding one of them to the Roof of his Mouth; and it is upon this Score, that when put into Water, Bubbles are raiſed by the Air in their Interſtices, which ſome have too fondly thought to be the Effects of their throwing out the Venom they had ſucked in.

Their *make* being thus, ſome Part at leaſt of the Poiſonous Juice may eaſily be

(*o*) *Diſſert. de Tarantula Hiſtor.*;
(*p*) *Pag.* 88.

drawn

drawn out of the Wound by fuch an Application, and yet fo much of *it* may fometimes happen to remain in the Flefh, as may make the Bite however to prove Mortal. And thus it fared with a Pigeon, to the Thigh of which, firft bitten by a Viper, I applied one of the Stones; for tho' it ftuck faft to the Wound, and thus faved the Life for about four Hours; (whereas others ufually died in about half an Hour) yet after this the Mortification of the Part prevailed to that Degree as to become fatal to the tender Creature.

But our *Viper-Catchers* have a Remedy far beyond all thefe, in which They do place fo great Confidence, as to be no more afraid of a Bite than of a common Puncture, immediately curing themfelves by the Application of their *Specifick*.

This, tho' they keep as a great Secret, I have however upon ftrict Enquiry found out to be no other than the *Axungia Viperina* prefently rubbed into the Wound. And to convince my felf of its good Effects, I inraged a Viper to bite a young Dog in the Nofe; both the Teeth were ftruck deep in; he howled bitterly, and the Part began to fwell; I diligently applied fome of the *Axungia*

I

I had ready at Hand, and he was very well the next Day.

But becaufe fome Gentlemen who faw this Experiment were apt to impute the Cure rather to the Dog's Spittle, (he licking the Wound) than to the Virtue of the *Fat*, we made him to be bit again in the Tongue, forbearing the Ufe of our Remedy, and he died within four or five Hours.

At another time I made the like Trial with the fame Succefs.

As this *Axungia* confifts of Clammy and Vifcid Parts, which are withal more Penetrating and Active than moft other Oily Subftances, *fo* thefe, without all doubt, do involve, and as it were fheath the Volatile Salts of the Venemous Liquor, and thus prevent their Shooting out into thofe Cryftalline *Spicula*, which we have obferv'd to be the main Inftruments of that deadly Mifchief which attends the Bite.

By this means it comes to pafs, that this Cure, if rightly manag'd, is fo eafie and certain, as not to need the help of any *Internal* Medicines to forward it ; but *Thefe* however muft take place, where, thro' Want of the other, the Poifon is

fpread

ſpread farther, and has tainted the whole Maſs of Blood.

Nor yet is it neceſſary even in this Caſe to fatigue the Patient with a *Farrago* of *Theriacas, Antidotes,* &c. for the *Volatile Salt* of Vipers is alone ſufficient to do the Work, if given in juſt Quantities, and duly repeated ; provided moderate Sweats be incouraged in Bed ; thus it ſucceeded with Monſieur *Charas* in the before cited Caſe, and in ſome others I could relate ; in one of which the Miſ-chief had gone ſo far as to induce an uni-verſal *Icterus.*

This leads me laſt of all to hint ſome-thing concerning the Uſe of the Viper in *Phyſick* ; becauſe Authors are very large in enumerating its Virtues againſt many, and thoſe too ſome of 'em very obſtinate, Diſtempers.

One of the firſt whom we find in An-tiquity to have made uſe of the Fleſh of this Creature to Medicinal Purpoſes, was, I think, *Antonius Muſa,* the Famons Phy-ſician to *Octavius Cæſar* ; of whom *Pliny (q)* tells us, That *when he met with incu-rable Ulcers, he ordered the eating of Vi-pers, and by this means they were quickly Healed.*

(q) *Lib.* 30. *c.* 13.

It

It is not improbable that he might have learned this from the Great *Greek* Physician *Craterus*, mention'd often by *Cicero* in his Epistles to *Atticus*, who, as *Porphyrius* (*r*) relates, *very happily cured a miserable Slave, whose Skin in a strange manner fell off from his Bones, by advising him to feed upon Vipers dressed after the manner of Fish,*

Be this as it will, in *Galen*'s time the profitable Qualities of the Viper were very commonly known; himself relating (*s*) very remarkable Stories of the Cures of the *Elephantiasis*, or *Lepra*, done by the Viper Wine.

Aretæus, who most probably liv'd about the same time with *Galen*, and of all the Ancients has most accurately described the *Elephantiasis*, commends, as *Craterus* did, the eating of Vipers instead of Fish in the same Diseases (*t*). And to this purpose I remember, that *as Lopes* (*u*) in his Relations of the Kingdom of *Congo* in *Africa*, takes notice how greedily the *Negroes* eat *Adders*, roasting them, and esteeming them as the most delicious Food; *so Dam-*

(r) *De Abstinent. ab animal.* lib. 1. p. m. 16.
(s) *De simpl. Medic. Facult.* lib. 11. c. 1.
(t) *Curat. Diuturn.* lib. 2. c. 13.
(u) *Vid. Purchas.* Pilgrims, Part 2. l. 7. c. 9.

pier

pier (x) alſo informs us, that the Natives of *Tonquin* in the *Eaſt Indies* do treat their Friends with *Arack,* in which *Snakes* and *Scorpions* have been infus'd, accounting this not only a great Cordial, but alſo an Antidote againſt the *Leproſie,* and all other ſorts of Poiſon.

The Phyſicians in *Italy* and *France* do very commonly preſcribe the Broth and Gelly of Vipers Fleſh for much the ſame Uſes, that is, to invigorate and purifie the Maſs of Blood exhauſted with Diſeaſes, or tainted with ſome Vicious and Obſtinate *Ferment.*

From all this it appears, That the main Efficacy of the Viperine Fleſh is to quicken the Circle of the Blood, promote its due Mixture, and by this means cleanſe and ſcoure the *Glands* of thoſe ſtagnating Juices, which, turning to Acidity, are the Origine of many, at leaſt, of thoſe troubleſome Diſtempers in the Surface of the Body, which go under the Names of *Scrophulous, Leprous,* &c.

Theſe good Effects are owing to that penetrating, ſtrong *Salt*, with which the Subſtance of theſe Creatures does, in a very great Proportion, abound; and the

---

Reafon of *this* is from the Food they live on, which we have obferv'd before to be Lizzards, Moles, *&c.* whofe Nature every one knows to be fuch as muft neceffarily, when they are diffolv'd in the Stomach, fupply the Blood with a great Quantity of Active and Volatile Parts. And herein lies the Difference between the Flefh of Vipers, and *that* of other Innocent Serpents, which feeding upon Grafs, Herbs, *&c.* do not recommend themfelves to us by any of thofe Properties which are in fo Eminent a Degree found in the former.

Whofoever reflects on what has been faid on this Head, will very readily Acknowledge, That our Phyficians deal too Cautioufly or Sparingly with a Remedy which may be apply'd to very good Purpofes, when they prefcribe a few Grains of the *Pouder* of dried Vipers, or make up a fmall Quantity of their Flefh into *Troches*; whereas, if Service be really to be done this Way, the Patient ought to eat frequently of Viper-Gelly, or Broth; or rather, as the ancient manner was, to boil Vipers, and eat them like Fifh; if this Food will not go down, (tho' really very Good and Delicious Fare) to make ufe at leaft of Wine, in which Vipers have for
a long

a long time been infused, by which I
know a very obstinate *Lepra* has been
removed; or lastly, in some Cases, especially where Wine is not Convenient,
to take good Quantities of their *Volatile
Salt*, in which alone the Virtue of the
before-named Medicines does principally
reside.

AN APPENDIX

TO THE

Foregoing Essay;

CONTAINING

Some Anatomical Observations on the VIPER, *and an Account of some other Venomous Animals.*

IN repeated Dissections of the *Viper,* comparing the *Descriptions* given Us by Authors with the *Parts* themselves, I have found them in many Particulars to be very Defective. I shall however at present confine my self to some Observations made chiefly on those Or-

gaus

gans which ferve to prepare and emit the *Poifon*.

To begin therefore with the Head. The *Skull* (*Fig.* 2.) is compofed of feveral Bones, joined together by *Sutures*, as in *Man*, but with this Difference, that the *Os Frontis* in the Viper confifts of Two Bones united by a Rectilinear *Suture*, and the *Parietal* Bones are entire ; whereas in Man the *Parietal* Bones have *Sutures*, and the *Os Frontis* is entire.

(*a*) Shews Two fmall Semicircular Bones, which form the inferior Part of the *Noftrils*.

(*b*) The Two Bones which make the upper Part of the *Nofe*, from the latter pafs down two thin *Laminæ*, which touching one another, and falling perpendicular upon the *Offa Palati*, compofe the *Septum* of the Nofe.

(*e e*) Point out the *Offa Frontis*, which form the upper Part of the *Orbits* of the Eyes. And (*c c*) the *Orbits* themfelves.

The *Parietal Bones* (*d*) make a large Cavity, in which the greateft Part of the Brain is contained, and *this* we may call the *Sinciput*.

Behind this Bone are placed the *Offa Temporum* (*ff*), in which lye the Or-

gans

gans of *Hearring* ; and behind Them a
Bone *(g)* which, we may call the *Os Occi-
pitis*, covers the pofterior Part of the
Brain. This is joined to the firft *Vertebra*
of the Neck *(h)*, by a Spherical Articulation, as all the *Vertebræ* are to one another ; and this is the Reafon why this
Creature can turn its Head and Body fo
.much, and fo nimbly, every way.

To fome of *Thefe* there are Two other
Bones Articulated for particular Ufes.

The Firft of *Them*, which ferves as a
Bafis to the Articulation of the Reft *(a,
Fig.* 4.), is faftned by one Extremity to
a fmall Proturberance *(i, Fig.* 2.) in the
middle and lateral Part of the *Os Sincipitis*, and running back towards the *Vertebræ*, lyes in the fame Plain with the
Sinciput. This Bone has a Motion, tho’
very inconfiderable, both upwards and
downwards. By means of This, the opening of the Mouth is fomewhat inlarged in
the Time of *Deglutition.*

That End of this Bone, which is next
to the *Vertebræ*, is articulated at oblique
Angles with *Another (b),* placed Hori-
zontally, and whofe Motion is forwards
and backwards, being made chiefly for
moving the Bones of the upper and lower
Jaw, into which the Teeth are inferted.

By reaſon of this kind of Articulation, It cannot contribute any thing towards widening the Mouth for Swallowing.

This Bone, and That with which it is joined, I call the *Common Bones.*

The *Upper Jaw* (*Fig.* 3.) is, beſides the Teeth, compoſed on each ſide of *three* Bones. The *Firſt* (*a*), into which the Poiſonous *Fangs* are fixt, is articulated with the Anterior Protuberance of the *Orbit* of the Eye ; and has a Motion of Flexion and Extenſion, that is, forwards and backwards, by which the *Fangs* are Erected or Depreſs'd. It is ſmall at the Joint, but grows broader by degrees, to a pretty large *Baſis,* the better to contain a conſiderable Number of *Teeth.* It is *Spongy* like the Subſtance of the *Vertebræ,* and no ways fit to be the immediate Organ of *Hearing,* as Mr. *Charas* and ſome others have imagined.

The *Second* (*c*), is a broad thin Bone, Articulated by *one* Extreme to the *Former,* (*f*), and by the *other* firmly fixt to the middle of the *third* Bone. When *this* is thruſt forwards, it likewiſe puſhes the *Firſt,* and by this means the *Erection* of the *Fangs* is helped ; and when it is pull'd backwards, they are *depreſſed.*

The

The *third* Bone (*e d*), is join'd by one Extremity (*e*), to the End of one of the Bones of the Lower Jaw (*c, Fig.* 4.), And being somewhat crooked, turns in a little towards the *Basis* of the *Cranium*, and running along the Inferior Part of it towards the *Nose*, terminates near the Internal and Anterior Part of the *first* Bone.

The *Lower Jaw* (*c d e f g, Fig.* 4.) on each side is made up of two Bones, but firmly united, the Extremity of the *one* entring within the *other* (*f*). The First (*c d e*) articulates with the Second of the *Common Bones* (*b*), where it is broad, and sends off an *Apophysis*, into which there is a *Muscle* inserted, which helps to open the *Jaw.* There is in *this* a *Hole* (*d*), for the Entrance of the Branch of the *Nerve*, which passing thro' a *Canal* in the middle of it, goes to the Extremity of the *Second* Bone, and in its way sends off several Branches which go to the *Teeth* ; and also a very considerable one, which goes out at (*e*), and is wholly spent upon the Neighbouring *Muscles.*

The *Second* Bone (*f g*) serves chiefly to receive the small *Teeth*, which answer to *those* in the upper Jaw.

As

As for the *Teeth*, they are of two Sorts, the *Great*, or poifonous *Fangs*, and the *Small*.

The *Great* (*b, Fig.* 3.), being fixt in the Firft Bone of the *Upper Jaw*, are Crooked and Bent, like the *Dentes Canini* in moft *Carnivorous* Animals. They are manifeftly hollow from their Root a confiderable way, not to the very *Apex* or Point, (which is folid and fharp, the better to pierce the Skin) but to a fmall diftance from it, as is plainly feen by fplitting the Tooth thro' the middle (*Vid. Fig.* 6.). This Cavity ends at the Convex Part in a vifible *Slit*, very well refembling the *Nip* or *Cut* of a *Pen* (*Fig.* 9. *d*), which is the *Emiffary* or Outlet to the Poyfon.

Galen (*a*) has given us a confiderable Hint of this Make of the Tooth : For, *The Mountebanks* (He fays) *ufed to fuffer themfelves to be bit by Vipers, having firft with fome Paftes ftopt the Holes of their Teeth, that the Venom being thus kept in, the Spectators might think they did by their Antidote fecure themfelves from its dangerous Effects.*

The Reafon why thefe Teeth are

(a) *De Theriac. ad Pifon.* Cap. 12.

Crooked,

Crooked, is, That the *Point* of the Tooth,
when the Viper bites, may be *Perpendicular* to the Part to be Wounded;
for the Head being raifed back in the
Time of Biting, and the Tooth erected,
if *this* were ftrait, It would not, by
reafon of its oblique Situation to the
Part, enter with fo much Force, nor fo
deep into the Flefh.

As for the *Number* of the Poifonous
Fangs, I have obferved, that there are,
for the moft part, befides One, Two or
Three on each fide, fixt Perpendicular-
ly to the firft Bone of the Upper Jaw,
fome others which are Young, and of
a fmaller Size, adhering to the fame Bone:
Their *Points* are hardened, and they
have their *Fiffures* formed as in the o-
ther, but their *Roots* are Soft and Mu-
cilaginous, like the Roots of the Teeth
in Infants, and fo they lye always deprefs'd at the *Bottoms* of the *Former*, as may
be feen *Fig.* 10. *c.*

They drop off from the Bone at the
leaft Touch; and therefore fome Anato-
mifts have imagined them to be faftened
to Mufcles or Tendons, which would
have rendred Them altogether Ufelefs.
For they are made to fupply the Place
of the *Greater*, when they fall away, or

are

are pulled out by Accident , and in order to do this, they do by degrees harden, and rife more and more, till at laft they ftand upright, and come to a Perpendicular Situation in the Bone.

They are not all of the fame *Growth*, for in fome we can only difcern the Shape of a Tooth without any Hardnefs, in *others* the Point, and in the *next* fomewhat more is hardened, and fo on to the greateft Fang.

Their Number is very uncertain, there being fometimes fix or feven in each fide of the Jaw, fometimes fewer.

Thefe feem to have occafioned the Difputes among the Ancients concerning the Number of the Viperine Teeth.

The Poyfonous Fangs have fmall Holes at the Internal Part of their Root, thro' which the Veffels pafs which carry their Nourifhment (*Fig.* 5. *a*).

It is remarkable, that Nature has provided Young Vipers with Poifonous Teeth grown to their Perfection, that fo they may kill their Prey as foon as they come into the World.

The *Second* Kind of Teeth, or the *Small*, are hooked, and bent, as well as the former, but without any *Slit* or Opening. Of Thefe there are Four Rows, Two on
each

each fide of the Mouth. They are fixt in the *third* Bone of the Upper Jaw, and in the *Second* in the Lower, as exhibited to view in the *Figures*.

Their Ufe is to hold the Prey faft while Execution is done by the Bite, left in ftruggling to get away, It fhould pull out the Fangs.

The Inftruments that *Emit* the Venom being thus defcrib'd, we come next to *thofe* which ferve to *Prepare* and *Contain* it.

This *Liquor* is feparated from the Blood by a *Gland* on each fide of the Head, placed in the Anterior and Lateral Part of the *Os Sincipitis,* juft behind the Orbit of the Eye (*Fig.* 9. *a*); It lies immediately under that Mufcle which helps to deprefs the Fangs, fo that by the Action of *this* it is Prefs'd; which is an admirable Contrivance to forward the *Secretion* of the Juice out of it.

'Tis a *Conglomerated* Gland, compofed of many fmaller ones contained in a common Membrane; each of Thefe fends off an Excretory Veffel, all which do afterwards Unite and Form one *Duct* (*b*), which running towards the Roots of the Fangs, difcharges the Yellow Liquor into a *Bag*.

This

This *Bag* is fixt to the *Basis* of the *first* Bone of the Upper Jaw, and also to the Extremity of the *Second*, covering the Fangs near the Root (*d, Fig.* 10.). To the upper Part of this *Vesicula* there is joined *another* (*a*), in the Anterior Part of which there is a Passage for the Poisonous Teeth.

This consists of Muscular Fibres, both. *Longitudinal* and *Circular,* by Means of which it can *Contract* it self when the Fangs are erected; and by this Contraction the *Venom* is pressʼd into the Hole at the Root of the Tooth, and forced out at the Fissure near the Point.

That this is so done, I have frequently observed with the naked Eye, having cut off the Head of a Viper, and immediately pinching the Neck to make it open the Mouth wide; for by this means the Venom was *Squirted* out as from a *Syringe.*

When the Viper lyes quiet with its Mouth shut, the Fangs are depressʼd and covered with the *External Bag*; when it intends to bite, it opens the Mouth very wide, at the same time the lower Extremity of the *Second* of the *Common* Bones (*Fig.* 4. *b*) is moved forwards by proper Muscles, and turns as it were upon the fixt

Centre

Centre (*b*), thus pushing forward the Upper and Lower Jaws, whose Extremes are united at (*c*). By this means the Lower Part of the First Bone of the Upper Jaw (*Fig. 3. a*) is thrust forwards, the other Extremity turning in the Cavity of its Articulation, where it is fastned by *Ligaments* ; the Fangs being by this Mechanism Erected, the Bags which covered them, by the Contraction of their *Longitudinal* Fibres, are pulled back, and the Action of the *Circular Ones* does at the same Time straiten the *Internal* Bag, and force the *Juice* into the Teeth.

Besides this, when the Viper bites, It strikes in the Fangs to the very Root ; and thus the *Vesiculæ* are still more squeezed for the Discharge of the Liquor.

It is worthy our Observation, that the Viper can move the Jaw Bones on *one* side without moving Those on the *other*, for they are not joined together at the Extremes as in other Animals ; which Contrivance is very beneficial to it in the *swallowing* its Prey ; in that, while the Teeth on one side stand unmoved, and fixt in the Flesh to hold it, *Those* on the other side are brought forward, to draw it in farther, then they keep it fast till the former Jaws advance again in their *Turn.*

Thus

Thus they act succeſſively, and force the Animal intire (there being no *Dentes Inciſivi* or *Molares* to divide it) into the *Œſophagus,* whoſe Muſcular Fibres are very Weak, and can help but little in the Buſineſs.

It may not be amiſs to conclude theſe *Remarks* with a a ſhort *Hint* concerning the *Organs of Hearing* ; Mr. *Charas* (who is however followed by others in *it*) having, as we mention'd before, Entertain'd a very abſurd Opinion about *Them.*

Theſe then are placed in the *Temporal* Bones, as in other Animals, and conſiſt of *One* long, ſmall *Bone* (*Vid.* Fig. 11.), like *that* of *Birds,* whoſe Extremity is broad, like the *Baſis* of the *Stapes* in *Man,* and ſituated upon a little *Hole* which opens into the *Labyrinth* ; and beſides of *three Demicircular Canals* (Fig. 12. *a b*) which alſo open into the *Labyrinth.*

This *Labyrinth* (**Fig. 13.**) has a great many *Eminencies* in it of no determin'd Regular Figure (*Fig.* 14.), and is covered with a *Membrane* full of *Nerves* and *Blood Veſſels.* The *Nerve* enters from the Brain at a Hole in the middle of this *Cavity* (*a,* Fig. 15.).

There

There is no *Cochlea* in the Ear of the Viper ; but the Anterior *Demicircular Canal* opens into a *Semicanal*, which makes fome *Spiral Turns* in the Fore-part of the *Labyrinth* ; in like manner as it is in *Fiſh.*

The *Paſſage* for the Air to theſe Organs. is not *Outward*, but, as in fome Fiſh, thro' the Mouth, between the Upper and Under Jaws, running below the *Second* of the *Common Bones.* But of *This*, and alfo of the True Mechanic *Uſe* of the aforefaid *Parts*, more hereafter.

Poisonous Animals.

AS the *Viper* is Hurtful by Inftilling a Liquid *Poifon* into the Wound made by its Teeth; fo likewife are all *Venomous* Creatures whatfoever, whether they *Bite* or *Sting*, tho' there be fome difference in the Contrivance of their *Organs*, Mifchievous after much the fame *Manner*; and moftly for the fame good *Ufe* and Purpofe, that is, in order to Kill their *Prey*.

This will fully appear, by Examining the *Inftruments* of Death in feveral of *Them*.

Firft then, The *Spider* which lives upon Flies, Wafps, and the like *Infects*, is provided with a hooked *Forceps*, placed juft by the Mouth, very fharp and fine; with *this* he pierces the Flefh of little Creatures caught in his *Webb*, and at the fame time infufes a *Juice* into the Puncture, by which means the Animal being Killed, He fucks out the Moifture from the Body, and leaves it a dry husky Carkafs.

Mr. *Van*

Mr *Van Leewenboek*, in his Account of *Spiders*, lately publifh'd *(a)*, has, together with the other Parts, by the help of his Glaffes, defcrib'd thefe *Weapons*, which He finds to lie couched on each fide the Mouth, in a Row of Teeth, till they are raifed to do Execution. Thefe Rows of Small *Teeth* are defign'd to hold the Prey, that It may not efcape the Force of the Bite. And in the Convex Part, towards the Point of each *Claw*, He has delineated a little Aperture or *Slit*, thro' which he fuppofes the Poifon iffues out at the fame time the Wound is made.

This *Situation* and *Motion* of thefe Parts, I have feveral times view'd; but was never able to difcern the *Exit* or Opening; which, having a juft Deference to the Induftry and Application of fo Nice an Obferver in Things of this Nature, I, at firft, imputed to my own Unskilfulnefs in fuch Enquiries, knowing my *Microfcope* to be very good; till at laft, after repeated Trials, I very plainly faw, That nothing dropt out of the *Claws*, which were always dry while the Spider Bit, but that a fhort, white *Probofcis* was at the fame time thruft out of the Mouth, which inftilled a *Liquor* into the Wound.

(a) *Philof. Tranfact.* N°. 271.

Then

Then I concluded, That Mr *Leewenhoek* had Delineated the *Apertures* in thefe *Weapons*, only from the *Analogy* which he thought they muft bear to the Viperine *Fangs*, the *Sting* of the *Scorpion*, *Bee*, &c. And I was confirmed in this Opinion by examining a *Claw* of the great *American* Spider, defcribed (tho' but lamely) by *Pifo* (*b*), and called *Nhamdu*; this was given Me by M^r. *Pettiver*, and being above fifty Times bigger than *that* of the largeft *Europæan* Spider (*c*), if there had been any Slit in it, my Glafs would no doubt have difcover'd it, but yet I found it to be quite Solid.

And indeed the Quantity of *Liquor* emitted by our common Spiders when they kill their Prey, is vifibly fo Great, and the wounding *Weapons* fo Minute, that they could contain but a very inconfiderable Portion thereof, if it were to be difcharged that Way.

To this purpofe, I remember Mr. *Boyle* fomewhere tells a Story of a Perfon blinded by a Spider dropping its Venom into his Eye, which tho' it can hardly find Credit with fome, is however confirmed by what *Pifo* relates of his *Nhamdu*, *Viz.*

(b) *Nat. Hift.* lib. 5. cap. 10.
(c) *Vid. Fig.* 18.

That

That in catching it great heed is to be taken, left its Poison fall into the *Eye*, This causing a total Loss of the *Sight*.

What Mr. *Leewenhoek* observes of the Enmity these Creatures bear to one another I have often seen; for if Four, Five, or more be put together into a Glass, they immediately fall to *Fighting* with all the Fury imaginable; *Limbs* struck off are usually the *Praeludes* to the terrible Slaughter, which continues till all are killed, the *Surviving Conqueror* himself most commonly Dying of his Wounds.

The *Weapons* of Mischief in the *Scolopendra* are much the same with Those of the Spider, only larger. One of these Creatures I had brought to Me alive out of a Ship which came from the *East-Indies*, where *Bontius* (*d*) says, Their Bite is so painful, that it makes People almost mad; but it died before I had an opportunity of making Trial of its Poison; however, I very diligently looked upon the Claws (*e*), and found them to have no more *Cavity* than is necessary for the Insertion of their Muscles, nor any *Exit* or Out-let towards

(d) *Hist. Ind.* p. m. 56.
(e) *Vid.* Fig. 17.

their

their *Apex* ; these therefore serve only to *pierce* the Flesh, and the Venom is infused from a *Proboscis* out of the Mouth ; tho' *This* I could not very well discern, because the Parts had been kept too long dry before I examined Them.

The Case is much the same with *Stinging* Animals ; of These the *Scorpion* is the Chief, whose *Virus* in different Countries is more or less dangerous, according as 'tis exalted by various Degrees of *Heat* ; thus in *Africa* particularly its Effects are so dreadful, that as *Joann. Leo* (f) tells Us, the Town of *Pescara* there is in a manner left desolate by the Inhabitants in the Summer Time, by Reason of the great Abundance of these Creatures, certain Death following their *Sting*.

Some of this deadly kind (the same, tho' not so large with *That* in the *East-Indies*, of which *Swammerdam* (g) has given a very accurate Description and Figure) Sr *Redi* had sent him from *Tunis* (b) ; and it being *November*, irritated them to *Sting* Pigeons, Pullets, &c. without any bad Effect at all of their *Poison* ; but upon the

(f) *Histor. Afric.* lib. 6.
(g) *Hist. Insect.* p. 147.
(h) *Generazione degli Inserti,* p. 15.

approaching Spring, One of them which had been kept all the Winter, nay, eight Months, without any Food, and the Wound of whose Sting before was harmless, stung to Death two Pigeons successively; but a Third and Fourth wounded in like manner, suffered no Hurt. Yet having let the *Scorpion* rest all Night, He killed another Pigeon the next Morning.

At the *Point* of the *Sting* he very often could discern a small drop of white *Liquor*, which when the Wound was made, entered into the Flesh.

As this *Liquid Venom* is either not separated from the Blood into the Cavity of the Sting, during the cold of Winter, or at least the Scorpion wants Strength at that Time to throw it out with Force and Energy. *So* even in the hot Months, after it is exhausted by two or three *Attacks*, the *Sting* is no longer hurtful, till the Expence of this *Juice* is recruited by Time.

'Tis very remarkable concerning this *Insect*, what an ingenious Gentleman who lived several Years in *Barbary* told Me, he had many times tried; That if it be surrounded with a Circle of *Burning Coals*, It does, upon the Sense of the *Heat*, turn it self violently every way to make an Escape; but finding it impossible, and

the

the *Pain* from the Fire increasing, it strikes it self Twice or Thrice with the *Sting* on the *Back*, and immediately dies of the Wounds.

Others may make what Reflections They please on this *Self-Murder*, it is to Me beyond all Dispute sufficient to decide the *Controversie* between Writers, whether Poisonous Animals of the same *Species* can kill each other. Which is not only confirmed by what we before observed of the *Spider*, but is likewise true of *Vipers*; for Dr. *Herman* bringing from the *Indies* Three of the *Cobras de Capelo* all in one Glass, Two of them were killed in the Voyage by *Fighting*.

As the *Viperine Venom* is the *Quintessence* and most active Part of those *Animal Juices* with which the Viper is nourished, so is also *That* of the Scorpion; for this Insect lives chiefly upon *Locusts*, &c. and the same Person from *Barbary* inform'd Me, That seeing oftentimes *Locusts* sticking up in the Ground as if they were *Set* there, by looking he found that some Part of them was always eat away, and that these Places were the *Holes* of Scorpions, who had dragg'd their Prey thither, and fed on it as they had Occasion.

In

In like manner, as the *Axungia Viperina* cures the Bite of the Viper, *so* also the *Oleum Scorpionum*, or Oil in which Scorpions have been infused, is a present Remedy for the Sting of this Creature.

The Mechanism of the Sting of a *Bee*, D^r. *Hooke* has very accurately described (*i*). One may with the naked Eye sometimes see it discharge the *Venom*; and in *this*, by the help of a *Glass*, I can easily discover a great Number of Minute *Salts* Floating.

And indeed this *Apparatus* or Contrivance is so universal, that we find even in *Vegetables* something Analogous hereunto; for the last mention'd Author (*k*), has shewn Us, That the pricking Points of *Nettles* do at the same time they pierce the Skin, instil a Venomous *Juice* into the Wound.

(i) *Micrograph. Observ.* 34.
(k) *Ibid. Obj.* 25.

ESSAY

ESSAY II.

OF THE

BITE

OF THE

TARANTULA

AND

MAD DOG.

I Join these Two *Poisons* together, because tho' they differ very much in
their Effects, yet both do agree in
this, that they induce a particular *Delirium
sui generis*, attended partly with *Maniacal,*

acal, partly with *Melancholy* Symptoms.

The *Tarantula* (of which the Figure may be seen in *Baglivi*'s Differtation (*a*),) is a *Spider* of *Apulia* of the *Octonocular* kind; that is of that *Species* that has eight Eyes, and fpins Webbs; it has eight Legs, four on each fide, and in each Leg three Joints; from the Mouth proceed two Darts, in Shape juft like to a hooked *Forceps*, or Crab's Claws; thefe are folid, and very fharp, fo that they can eafily pierce the Skin; and between thefe and the Fore-Legs there are two little Horns, which I fuppofe do anfwer to thofe Bodies call'd from their Ufe in *Flies* the *Feelers*; becaufe as they do, fo this Creature is obferved to move 'em very briskly when it approaches to its Prey.

This, as other Spiders do, propagates its *Species* by laying Eggs, which are very numerous; fo that there are found fometimes in the Female, when diffected, a hundred or more; and thefe are hatched partly by the Heat of the Mother, partly by that of the Sun, in about twenty or thirty Days Time.

(*a*) *De Tarantul.*

There

There is also a Spider of the like Nature with the *Tarantula* in the *West-Indies*, which *Fr. Hernandez* (*b*) describes by the Name of *Hoitztocatl*, or the *Pricking Spider* ; and says, that its Bite induces Madness.

In the Summer Months, especially when the Heats are greatest, as in the Dog-Days, the *Tarantula* creeping among the Corn in the Fields, bites the Mowers and Passengers ; in the Winter it lurks in Holes, and is scarcely seen ; and if it does bite then, it is not venomous, neither does it induce any ill Symptoms.

But in the hot Weather, altho' the Pain of its Bite is at first no greater than what is caused by the Sting of a Bee, yet the Part quickly after is discoloured with a Livid, Black, or Yellowish Circle, and raised to an inflam'd Swelling ; the Patient within a few Hours is seized with a violent Sickness, Difficulty of Breathing, universal Faintness, and sometimes Trembling, with a Weakness of the Head ; being asked what the Ail is, makes no Reply, or with a querulous Voice, and melancholy Look, points to his Breast, as if the Heart was most affected.

(*b*) *Histor. Animal. Nov. Hispan.* Tract. 4. c. 5.

During this mournful Scene, all the usual *Alexipharmick* and *Cordial* Medicines are of no Service ; for notwithstanding their repeated Use, the Patient growing by degrees more melancholy, stupid, and strangely timorous, in a short Time expires, unless *Musick* be called to his Assistance, which alone, without the Help of Medicine, performs the *Cure*.

For at the first Sound of the *Musical Instrument*, altho' the Sick lie, as it were, in an Apoplectick Fit, they begin by Degrees to move their Hands and Feet, till at last they get up, and fall to Dancing with wonderful Vigour, at first for three or four Hours, then they are put to Bed, refreshed from their sweating, for a short time, and repeat the Exercise with the same Vehemence, perceiving no Weariness or Weakness from it, but professing they grow stronger and nimbler the more they dance.

At this Sport they usually spend Twelve Hours a Day, and it continues Three or Four Days ; by which time they are generally freed from all their Symptoms, which do nevertheless attack 'em again about the same time the next Year ; and if they do not take Care to prevent this Relapse by Musick, they fall into

into a *Jaundice,* Want of Appetite, univerfal Weaknefs, and fuch like Difeafes;
which are every Year increafed, if Dancing be neglected, till at laft they prove
incurable.

As Mufick is the common *Cure,* fo they
who are bitten are pleas'd fome with one
Sort of it, fome with another; one is raifed with a Pipe, another with a Tymbrel;
one with a Harp, another with a Fiddle;
fo that the Muficians make fometimes feveral Effays before they can accommodate
their Art to the Venom; but this is conftant and certain, notwithftanding this
Variety, that they all require the quickeft
and briskeft Tunes, and are never moved by
a flow, dull *Harmony.*

While the *Tarantati,* or Affected, are
Dancing, they lofe in a manner the Ufe
of all their Senfes, like fo many Drun-
kards, do many Ridiculous and Foolifh
Tricks, talk and act obfcenely and
rudely, take great Pleafure in playing
with Vine-Leaves, with naked Swords,
red Cloths, and the like; and on the
other Hand can't bear the Sight of any
thing black; fo that if any By-ftander
happen to appear in that *Colour,* he muft
immediately withdraw, otherwife they
relapfe

relapfe into their Symptoms with as much Violence as ever.

It may afford fome Light towards Underftanding the Nature of this Poifon, to obferve that *Apulia* is the hotteft Part of all *Italy*, lying *Eaftward*, and having all the Summer long but very little Rain to temper the Heats, fo that the Inhabitants, as one of that Country obferves (c), do breath an Air, as it were, out of a fiery Furnace; hence their Temperament is dry, and aduft, as appears by their being generally lean, paffionate, impatient, ready to Action, quick-witted, very fubject to inflammatory Diftempers, Phrenfies, Melancholy, and the like, upon which Account there are more mad People in this, than in all the other Parts of *Italy*; nay, what in other Countries is but a light Melancholy, arifes here to a great Heigth; for Women in a *Chlorofis* do fuffer almoft the fame Symptoms as Perfons poifoned by the *Tarantula* do, and are cured the fame Way; and in like manner the Venom of the *Scorpion* does here in Effects and Cure agree very much with that of this *Spider*.

(c) *Baglivi*, p. 11.

From

From all this Hiftory it fufficiently appears, that thofe that are bitten by a *Tarantula*, do thereupon become *Delirous*, and that in order to account for their furprizing Symptoms ; the Nature of a *Delirium*, from which many of them proceed, ought to be underftood

Such is the Conftitution of the *Human OEconomy*, that *as* upon the Impreffion of outward *Objects* made upon the *Organs*, and by the Fluid of the Nerves conveyed to the *Common Senfory* ; different *Species* are excited there, and reprefented to the Mind ; *fo* likewife upon this Reprefentation, at the Command and Pleafure of the Soul, part of the fame Fluid is determin'd into the Mufcles, and mixing with the Arterial Blood there, performs all the Variety of Voluntary Motions and Actions.

This Order has been always fo conftant in Us, that at length by a kind of natural Habitude, without the Intervention of the Reafoning Faculty, Reprefentations made to the Mind do immediately and neceffarily produce fuitable Motions in the Bodily Organs. When therefore thefe Reprefentations are irregular, the Actions onfequent to them muft neceffarily be fo oo.

F   This

This being premis'd, it may perhaps be probably faid, that a *Delirium* is the Reprefentation and various Compofition of feveral *Species* to the Mind, without any Order or Coherence; together, at leaft moft commonly, with irregular, or, as it were, undefigned Motions of the Body; that is, fuch a wandring and irregular Motion of the Nervous Fluid, whereby feveral Objects are reprefented to the Mind, and upon this Reprefentation divers Operations perform'd by the Body, tho' thofe Objects are not imprefs'd upon the Organs, nor thofe Operations or Motions deliberately commanded by the Soul.

The Mind indeed is the firft Principle of all Mufcular Motion; but in fuch Cafes as thefe, its Promptitude to Action or Habit being fo great, it is in a manner furpriz'd, and cannot recover it felf after the Spirits are with violent Force determin'd purfuant to the Reprefentation of the *Species*. For, *as* in the former State of Things a Man is faid to act Rationally, *fo* this latter Cafe is call'd a *Perturbation of Mind*, that is, a *Delirium*; tho' it is very manifeft, that in reality the Defect is not in the *Rational*, but *Corporeal* Part; fuch *Species* being really prefented to the Mind, upon which by the Order of our
Con-

Conftitution fuch Motions ought to follow in the Body.

Thus, for Inftance, if the Liquor of the Nerves is, without the Prefence of any thing hurtful, put into a Motion like unto that which a painful Impreffion makes in it, the fame Bodily Actions muft infue as proceed from Fear, Anger, or the like Paffion, determining the Spirits towards the Mufcular Parts; and a By-ftander, who fees no reafon for fuch a Reprefentation made to the Mind, will prefently conclude that the Perfon thus acting acts without or befides his Reafon, that is, is *Delirous*; efpecially if the Hurry and Confufion of the Spirits be fuch, that not only *one*, but *feveral* different *Species* be at the fame time prefented to the Mind; for a Man in this Cafe may act the Part of one Joyful, Angry, Timorous, or the like, without any appearing Reafon, and all this almoft in the fame Moment of Time.

In one Word, *Deliria* are the *Dreams* of thofe who are *Awake*; and *as thefe* in Us *Sleeping* are infinitely various and wonderfully Compounded, and all from the fame common *Caufe*, diverfely preffing the Orifices of the Nerves, and thus making different *Repercuffions* of their

F 2 Fluid;

Fluid ; and *as* we all know that this Confufion making the Reprefentation of feveral *Species* to the Mind, there do here-upon follow, tho' the Body feem now at Reft and in perfect Repofe, fuch Mo-tions in the Organs as are ufually the Ef-fect of the Arbitrary Determination of the Spirits thither ; *fo* We are now to enquire what Alteration of the Body made by this Venom, can be the Occafion of this Dif-order and Tumult in the Nervous Fluid, which excites in the Party infected fuch furprizing, and almoft contradictory, Re-prefentations.

Moft of the Symptoms of thofe who are bitten by the *Tarantula* are at the firft, that is, before they rife to a *Delirium*, plainly the fame with thofe which the Bite of a Viper induces ; without doubt therefore, as we have before obferved of the common Spider, that it pierces the Flefh with its hooked *Forceps*, and at the fame time inftils from the *Probofcis* in the Mouth a liquid Venom into the Wound ; fo the like *Claws* in *This* (of which I have taken the Figure (*a*) out of *P. Bonanni*, very much magnified (*b*),) do ferve to

---

(a) *Vid. Fig.* 16.
(b) *Micrograph. Curiof.* p. 69.

make

make Way for an active and penetrating Juice emitted from the fame Part.

Of the Nature of which we may probably conjecture, that it is, when mixed with the Blood, being exalted by the Heat of the Climate, of fo great Force and Energy, that it immediately raifes an extraordinary Fermentation in the whole Arterial Fluid, by which its Texture and *Crafis* is very confiderably altered ; the Confequent of which Alteration, when the Ebullition is over, muft neceffarily be a Change in the *Cohæfion* of its Parts, by which the *Globules*, which did before with equal Force prefs each other, have now a very differing and irregular *Nifus* or Action, fo that fome of 'em do fo firmly cohere together, as to compofe *Molecula*, or fmall Clufters ; upon which Account there being now a greater number of *Globules* contained in the fame Space than before, and befides, the *Impulfe* of many of thefe when united together differing according to the Conditions of their *Cohæfion*, as to Magnitude, Figure, *&c.* not only will the *Impetus*, with which this Fluid is drove towards the Parts, be at fome Strokes at leaft greater than ordinary ; but the Preffure upon the Blood Veffels muft be

very

very unequal and irregular; and this more especially will be felt in them which are moft eafily diftended; fuch are thofe of the Brain, &c. And hereupon the Fluid of the Nerves muft neceffarily be put into various *Undulatory* Motions, fome of which will be like unto thofe which different *Objects* acting upon the Organs or Paffions of the Mind, do naturally excite in *It*, whereupon fuch Actions muft follow in the Body, as are ufually the Confequents of the feveral *Species* of Sadnefs, Joy, Defpair, or the like Determinations of the Thoughts; and we fhall readily pronounce one in this Condition, *Sad, Joyful, Timorous, &c.* and all without any apparent Reafon or Caufe; that is, in one Word, we fhall fay he is *Delirous*.

This is in fome Degree a *Coagulation* of the Blood, which will the more certainly, when attended with an extraordinary Heat, as in the prefent Cafe, produce fuch like Effects as thefe, becaufe the *Spirits* feparated from the Blood thus Inflamed, and Compounded of hard, fixt and dry Particles, muft unavoidably fhare in this Alteration; that is, whereas their Fluid confifts of two Parts, *One* more active and

and Volatile, the *Other* more Viſcid and Glutinous, which is a kind of Vehicle to the former; their *Active* Part will bear too great a Proportion to the *Viſcid*; and thus they muſt neceſſarily be of more than ordinary Volatility and Force, and will therefore, upon the leaſt Occaſion imaginable, be irregularly determin'd to every Part; and hereupon will follow Tremblings of the Body, Anger or Fear upon a light or no Cauſe, extream Pleaſure at what is but a Trivial Entertainment, as Red, Green Colours, or the like; and on the other hand, wonderful Sadneſs at any thing not agreeable to the Eyes, as dark and black Things; nay, ridiculous Laughter, obſcene Talk and Actions, and ſuch like Symptoms; becauſe in this Conſtitution of the Nervous Fluid, the moſt light Occaſion will make as real a *Reflux* and *Undulation* of it to the Brain; that is, will preſent as lively and vivid *Species* there, as the ſtrongeſt Cauſe and Impreſſion can produce in its natural State and Condition; nay, in ſuch a Confuſion, the Spirits cannot but ſometimes, without any manifeſt Cauſe at all, be hurried towards thoſe Organs, to which at other times they have

F 4   been

been moſt frequently determined ; and every one knows which they are in hot Countries and Conſtitutions.

We muſt however here remember what in the former Eſſay we mention'd of the Fluid of the Nerves, being *immediately* altered by the venomous Juice.

It will perhaps make this Theory more than probable, to conſider that *Baglivi* (*a*), in the Diſſection of a *Rabbit* kill'd by a *Tarantula,* found the Blood Veſſels of the Brain very turgid, and the Subſtance of the Brain it ſelf, that is, the Beginning of the Nerves, lightly inflamed, and with livid Spots here and there, the *Lungs* and other *Viſcera* diſtended, with concrete glotted Blood, and large Grumes of Blood with *Polypous* Branches in the Heart, a large Quantity of extravaſated *Serum* upon the Brain, which is (as he takes Notice) moſtly obſerved in thoſe Subjects which died by a Coagulation of the Blood.

Neither is it amiſs to remark, that in a *Chloroſis* there is nothing preternatural but an *infarctus* of the Arteries, and hence a retarded *Circulation,* from an Evacuation ſuppreſs'd ; and in this Country too much Heat ; that is, a beginning

(*a*) Pag. 40.

Coagu-

Coagulation, together with an Inflammatory Difpofition.

In fhort, *Bellini* has at large demonftrated, how *Deliria,* as well as *Melancholic* as *Manaical,* do proceed from a State of the Blood and Spirits, not unlike to that I have here defcribed.

But no lefs a Confirmation of thefe Notions may we have from the *Cure*; as to which it is obfervable, that the *Tarantati* have no Inclination to *dance* before they hear the Mufick; for being ask'd to do it, they anfwer, it is impoffible, they have no Strengh.

As for the Reafon therefore of their ftarting up at the firft Noife of the Inftrument, we muft reflect upon what we have juft now been faying concerning the Caufe of the Motions of the Body in a *Delirium*; and confider withal, that mufcular Motion is no other than a Contraction of the Fibres from the Arterial Fluid making an Effervefcence with the Nervous Juice, which by the light Vibration and Tremor of the Nerve, is derived into the Mufcle.

And thus we have a twofold Effect and Operation of Mufick, that is, both upon the Mind and Body. For a brisk Harmony excites lively *Species* of *Joy* and

Gladnefs,

Gladneſs, which are always accompany'd with a more frequent and ſtronger Pulſe, or an increaſed influx of the Liquor of the Nerves into the Muſcles, upon which ſuitable Actions muſt immediately follow ; and if we remember what we before hinted, that People in this Country are ſprightly and ready to Exerciſe, and that in ſuch a ſtate of the Fluids as we have deſcrib'd, a ſlight Occaſion preſents as ſtrong *Species*, as a greater can at another time : The Influence of Muſick on the *Mind* will appear to be ſo much the more powerful and certain.

As for the *Body*, ſince it is ſufficient for the purpoſe of putting the Muſcles into Action, to cauſe thoſe *Tremors* of the Nerves by which their Fluid is alternately dropt into the moving Fibres ; it is all one whether this be done by the determination of the Will, or the outward *Impulſions* of of an *Elaſtic* Fluid ; ſuch is the *Air* ; and that Sounds are the *Vibrations* of It, is beyond diſpute.

Theſe therefore rightly modulated may ſhake the Nerves as really as the *Imperium Voluntatis* can do, and conſequently produce the like Effects.

That This is ſo, beſides what we ſhall add anon, we may be convinced by a
Story

Story which M^r. *Boyle* (*a*) relates out of *Scaliger*, of a Knight of *Gascony* whom the sound of a *Bagpipe* would unavoidably force to make Water ; for this Secretion we know is regularly the Effect of an Arbitrary Contraction of the Muscle of the Bladder.

The obstinate continuing of the *Tarantati* in this Exercise, is doubtless in a great Measure owing to the strong Opinion they have of receiving Advantage from it, being incouraged by the Bystanders, and having always believed, and been told, that it was the only Cure in these Cases.

The *Benefit* from Musick is not only their Dancing to It, and so evacuating by *Sweat* a great Part of the Inflammatory Fluid ; but besides this, the repeated Percussions of the Air hereby made, by immediate Contact shaking the Contractile Fibres of the Membranes of the Body, especially those of the Ear, which being continuous to the Brain, do communicate their Tremblings to its Membranes and Vessels ; by these continued Succussions and Vibrations, the *Cohæsion* of the Parts of the Blood is perfectly broken, and its

(*a*) Of Languid and unheeded Motion.

Coagulation

Coagulation prevented ; fo that the Heat being removed by Sweating, and the Coagulation by the Contraction of the Mufcular *Fibrillæ*, the wounded Perfon is reftored to his former Condition.

If any one doubts of this force of the *Air*, let him confider that it is in *Mechanics* (*b*) Demonftrated, that the fmalleft *Percuffion* of the fmalleft Body, can overcome the refiftance of any great Weight which is in Reft ; and that the Languid Tremor of the Air, which is made by the Sound of a Drum or Trumpet, may fhake the vafteft and ftrongeft Edifices.

But befides all this, We muft allow a great deal to the *determinate Force*, and particular *Modulation*, of thefe trembling Percuffions ; for contractile Bodies may be acted upon by one certain Degree of Motion in the ambient Fluid, tho' a greater Degree of it differently qualified may produce nothing at all of the like Effect ; this is not only very apparent in the common Experiment of Two String'd Mufical Inftruments tuned both to the fame Heigth, the Strings of the one being ftruck upon, thofe of the other will found, and yet a much greater Motion of the Air

(*b*) *Borelli De Vi Percuffion.* Prop. 90, *and* 111.

may

may not Caufe any fenfible Vibration at all in the fame Chords; but alfo by the *Trick* which many have of finding the Tone or Note peculiarly belonging to any *Wine Glafs*, and by accommodating their *Voice* exactly to that Tone, and yet making it loud and lafting, they will make the Veffel tho' not touch'd, firft to Tremble, and then Burft; which it will not do if their Voice be but a little either too low or too high.

This laft Confideration makes it no very difficult matter to conceive the reafon, why different Perfons, infected with this Venom, do require oftentimes a different fort of Mufick in order to their Cure, in as much as their Nerves and *Diftractile* Membranes have differing *Tenfions*, and confequently are not in like manner to be acted upon by the fame *Vibrations*.

Nor are We to wonder at the Oddnefs of this Method and Practice; for *Mufick*, altho' it be Now-a-days applied to quite different Purpofes, was anciently made great Ufe of for the removing of many, and thofe too fome of the moft difficult and obftinate Difeafes.

For this we have a Famous Teftimony in *Galen* himfelf, (*a*) who tells us, that

(*a*) *De Sanitate Tuenda*, lib. 1. c. 8.

Æfculapius

Æsculapius used to recover Those in whom violent Motions of the Mind had induced a hot Temperament of Body, by Melody and Songs. Pindar (*b*) mentions the same thing; and indeed from hence not only the Notion, but the very Name of *Charming* (*c*) seems to have taken its Origine. *Athenæus* (*d*) relates that *Theophrastus* in his Book of *Enthusiasm* says, *Ischiadic Pains are Cured by the Phrygian Harmony.* This sort of Musick was upon a *Pipe*, and the most vehement and brisk, of all the Ancients knew; so that indeed it was said to raise those who heard it to downright Fury and Madness (*e*) : And such we have observed to be required to the Venom of the *Tarantula.*

But what is besides in this last Authority very observable to our Purpose, is the manner of using this Remedy, and that was (*f*) by *Playing upon the part affected,* which confirms what we have just now advanced concerning the Effect of the *Percussion* of the Air upon the Con-

---

(*b*) *Pythior. Od. 3.* μαλακαῖς ἐπαοιδαῖς. *Vid. ibid. Scholia.*
(*c*) *A Carmine.*
(*d*) *Deipnosoph.* l. 14. p. m. 624.
(*e*) *Vid. Bartholin. de Tibiis Veter.* l. 1. c. 9.
(*f*) ἀ καταυλῆσοι ἴὶς τῦ τότε ἴῆ φρυγισὶ ἁρμονίᾳ.

tractile

tractile Fibres of the *Brain*, for *Piping up-on* any Member of the Body, cannot be suppos'd to do Service any other way, than by such Succussions and Modulated Vibrations as we before mention'd. And this indeed *Cælius Aurelianus* (*a*) agrees to, who calls this Practice, *Decantare Loca dolentia*; and says, that the *Pain is mitigated and discuss'd by the Tremblings and Palpitations of the Part.*

Aulus Gellius (*b*) not only relates this same Cure of *Ischiadic* Ails as a thing notorious enough, but adds besides out of *Theophrastus*, that *the Musick of a Pipe rightly managed healed the Bites of Vipers.*

And not only does *Apollonius* (*c*) mention the Cure of Distractions of the Mind, Epilepsies, and several other Distempers this same way; but *Democritus* (*d*) in his Treatise of Plagues, taught, that *the Musick of Pipes was the Medicine for most Diseases*; which *Thales* of *Crete* confirmed by his Practice, when sent for by the *Lacedæmonians* to remove from them

(*a*) *Morb. chronic. l. 5. c. 1. Quæ cum saltum sumerent pal-pitando discusso dolore mitescerent.*
(*b*) *Noct. Atticar. l. 4. c. 13.*
(*c*) *Histor. Mirabil.*
(*d*) *Apud Aul. Gell. loc. citat. Plurimis hominum Morbis Medicinam fuisse Incentiones Tibiarum.*

the

the Peftilence, he did it by the help of Mufick (e).

All which Inftances do evince this Remedy to have been very ancient in many Cafes; and indeed as *Cælius Aurelianus (f)*, takes notice that the firft ufe of it was afcrib'd to *Pythagoras* himfelf, fo He having fettled and founded his Sect in thofe very Parts of *Italy* which are the Country of the *Tarantula*, going then under the Name of *Græcia magna*, now *Calabria*; it is not, I think, at all improbable that he may have been the Author and Inventor of this Practice there, which has continued ever fince. Efpecially fince *Jamblichus* affirms (g,). not only that he made ufe of Mufick in Phyfick, but particularly that he found out and contrived fome Harmonies to eafe the Paffions of the Mind, and others for the *Cure of Bites:* But of Mufick enough.

To conclude with this Poifon, we may take notice that, as to the *Return* of the Symptomes the next Year, That is owing to the fame exceffive Heat in thofe Months,

---

(e) *Plutarc. de Mufica.*
(f) *Loc. ante cit.*
(g) *De Vit. Pythagor. cap.* 25. πρὸς δηγμὸς Βοηϑηlικώτατα μέλη.

acting

acting again upon the small remains of the Venomous *Ferment* ; thus *Bartholin* (*i*) relates a Story of a Melancholy Phyfician at *Venice*, who fuffer'd the Attacks of his Difeafe only during the Dog-days, which yearly ended and return'd with them. A convincing proof how great a fhare Heat has in all thefe Cafes.

(*k*) *Hiftor. Anatom.* Cent. 2. H. 26.

Of the Mad DOG.

MORE difficult and terrifying are the Symptoms from the Bite of a *Mad Dog*, whose Venom has this also surprising in it, that the bad Effects do not appear oftentimes till the Cause of 'em is forgot; for the Wound is as easily cured as a common Bite is; but nevertheless a considerable time after, a melancholy Tragedy succeeds, sometimes sooner, sometimes later; for there are Instances of its being deferred to Two, (*k*) Six Months, nay, a Year, and longer, tho' the attack is generally within Forty Days after the Wound; about that time, the Patient complains of Running Pains all over his Body, especially near the Part wounded, like unto those in a Rheumatism, grows pensive and sad, prone to Anger upon little or no Occasion, with an intermitting Pulse, Tremblings and Contractions of the

(*k*) S. *Ardoyn de Venen*. pag. 381.

Nerves,

Nerves, with a great inward Heat and Thirst; and yet in a few Days (when the Disease is come to its height) a Dread and Fear of Water, and any Liquor whatsoever; so that at the very sight of it he falls into dismal Convulsions and Agonies, and cannot drink the least drop; and this *Hydrophobia*, or *Aquæ Timor*, has been always accounted the surest Sign and Mark of this Poison, as distinguishing it from all others.

The Ancients have at large described these Symptoms, as *Galen*, *Dioscorides*, *Aetius*, *Ægineta*, but most particularly of all, *Cælius Aurelianus* (*a*); and later Writers have given us several Instances of the *Hydrophobia*; Two Histories of it published, the one by Dr. *Lister* (*b*), the other by Dr. *Howman* (*c*), I shall more especially take Notice of, and refer to, as containing the most exact and large Account of any I have met with; he that desires more, may consult the several Authors cited by that diligent Observer, *Stalpart van der Wiel* (*c*).

(*a*) *De Morb. Acut.* lib. 3.
(*b*) *Exercitat. de Hydrophob.*
(*c*) Philosoph. Transact. N°. 169.
(*c*) *Observ. Rarior. Centur.* 2. obs. 100.

That this Difeafe is accompany'd with a *Delirium*, is almoft the common Opinion both of Ancients and Moderns ; *Damocrates* called it the barking Phrenfie (*e*); but Dr. *Lifter* agrees in this Point with *Petrus Salius Diverfus* (*f*), and will not allow a *Delirium* to be the neceffary confequent of this Venom ; and yet at the fame time he tells us, that his Patient barked like a Dog, and bit at the By-ftanders ; that he threw into his Mouth what was given him more haftily and fuddenly than it is Natural or Cuftomary for Men to do.

From fuch Actions as thefe, together with thofe mentioned before in relating the Symptoms, it is obvious enough to conclude, that Perfons thus affected are in a proper Sence *Delirous*. Tho' at the fame time I do think that the *Hydrophobia* it felf (whatever is commonly believed) does not at all proceed from this *Delirium*, as will by and by appear.

(*d*) *Vid. Galen. de Theriac. ad Pifon,* l. 1. cap. 16.
(*e*) Παρακοπὴν ὑλακτικὴν, *apud Galen de Antidot.* lib. 2. cap. 15.
(*f*) *De Hydroph.*

I

I know indeed that the main and plaufible *Objection* againft a *Delirium* is this, that the Patient himfelf does Reafon againft his Timoroufnefs, tho' he cannot overcome it, forewarns the Standers-by of his Outrageous Fits, defires them to take care of themfelves, and the like. Which from what I have already faid concerning a *Delirium*, appears to be very confiftent with it, nay, convinces that there is the greateft Degree of it in this Cafe; in as much as that it is not a Diftemper of the Mind but of the Body. And to this purpofe I remember to have feen my felf an Inftance of one in a Fever, who foretold fome time before any figns of a *Delirium* were difcovered, how raving and unruly He fhould be, and made good his *Prognoftick* to that degree, that it was very hard Work to tame and mafter him; tho', as he told me afterwards, he reafon'd as much as he could againft that groundlefs Jealoufie of his Friends defigning to Murder him, which put him upon his Mad Actions, but was not able to Conquer the prevailing *Species* of Fear and Anger.

This

This *Delirium* therefore, as *Cælius Aurelianus* (g) says, *Proceeds intirely from an indisposition of the Body,* which is without all doubt owing to the alteration made in the Blood by the *Saliva* of the *Mad Dog,* instill'd into the Wound inflicted by the Bite.

That we may rightly understand this, we must take Notice, that the *Rabies* or Madness in a Dog is the effect of a Violent Fever; and therefore it is most common in excessive Hot Weather, tho' sometimes intense Cold may be the Cause of it; That no Dog in this Case ever sweats; from whence it follows, that when his Blood is in a Ferment, it cannot, as in other Creatures, discharge it self upon the surface of the Body, and therefore must of necessity throw out a great many *Saline* and Active Particles upon those Parts, where there is the most constant and easie Secretion; and such, next to the *Miliary* in the Skin in Us, are the *Salival* Glands; for this reason much more Spittle is separated in a Dog when Mad, than at any other time, and that very frothy, or impregnated with Hot, Subtil Parts.

(g) *Loc. citat. Tota oritur ex Corporis ipsius mala Affectione.*

Now

Now as we every Day obferve, that what is thrown out from Liquors in a Ferment, is capable of inducing the like Motion in another Liquor of the fame kind, when duly mixed with it; fo we may very well fuppofe in the prefent Cafe, that the *Saliva*, which is it felf one of the moft Fermentative Juices in Nature, being turgid with Fiery, Saline Particles thrown into it out of the boiling Blood, when it comes by means of a Wound to be Incorporated with the Arterial Fluid of any One, does by Degrees raife a preternatural Effervefcence in it; the Effects of which will neceffarily be moft felt in thofe Parts which being tender, are the leaft able to refift the diftenfion of the Blood Veffels; fuch are the Stomach, and efpecially the Brain; and hereupon *Deliria*, with *Maniacal*, and fuch like Symptoms, will eafily infue.

A Perfon thus affected may be faid in a Degree to have put on the *Canine* Nature, tho' his Reafon be all this time untouch'd and intire, may Bite, Howl, &c. becaufe the *like* violent Agitation of the Blood in Him as was in the Dog will prefent like *Species*, and confequently (fo far as their different Natures will allow). produce like Actions; juft as it has been ob-

G 4

ferved,

ferved, that *Sheep* bitten by a Mad Dog, have run at the Shepherd like fo many Dogs to Bite him ; fo much can an Alteration of the Blood and Spirits do. And as a Timorous Creature may be imboldened, fo we oftentimes fee Perfons Courageous enough by a change made in the Blood by Evacuations, that is, by want of Force and Motion in that Fluid, made fheepifh Cowards, in defpight of their Reafon, fo long as that Defect is continued.

But the main difficulties in this matter are, the Mifchief difcovering it felf fo long after the Bite, and the *Hydrophobia.*

As to the former, we are to confider, that Fermentation being a Change made in the Cohæfion of the compounding Parts of a Fluid, it is fometimes a longer, fometimes a fhorter time before this Alteration is wrought; which variety may proceed either from the different Nature and Conftitution of the Ferment, or of the Liquor Fermented, and a great Number of Circumftances befides. So that this Venom may be all the while doing its Work, tho' the change made by it may not be fo confiderable as to be fenfibly taken Notice of till a long time after.

Nay,

Nay, it may fo happen, that the *Ferment* being Weak may not raife in the Blood any remarkable Agitation at all, till fome accidental Alteration in the Body un-luckily gives it an additional Force. As we before obferved, how much external Heat concurrs to heighten the Symptoms from the Bite of the *Tarantula*. And this probably may be the Cafe of Thofe in whom this Malignity has not appear'd till Six, or Twelve Months after the Wound.

That we may underftand the Reafon of the *Hydrophobia*, it is to be Remarked, that this dread of Water does not come on till the latter end of the Difeafe, Three or Four Days before Death ; that is, not till this preternatural *Fermentation* in the Blood is come to its Heigth ; and as in the Dog, fo in the Patient, a great quantity of Fermentative Particles is thrown off upon the Glands of the Mouth and Stomach, as appears by his Foaming at the Mouth, *&c.*

As alfo, that this *Fear* is not from a fight *of*, or any imaginary appearance *in* the Water, for if the Veffel be clofe fhut, and the Patient bid to fuck thro' a Quill, as foon as he has tafted, he falls into An-guifh and Convulfions, as Dr. *Lifter* ob-ferved. It is therefore highly probable,

if

if not certain, that this furprifing Symptom proceeds from the intolerable *Pain* which any Liquor at this time taken induces, partly by hurting the inflamed Membranes of the *Fauces* in Deglutition ; partly by fermenting with thefe Active Particles difcharged by the Blood upon the *Sto-machic* Glands, and thus twitching and irritating the Nervous Membranes ; the very memory of which *grievous Sence*, after it is once felt, is fo terrible, that the affe-cted Perfon chufes any thing rather than to undergo it a fecond time.

The Effects of this *Irritation* are mani-feft in the Convulfions of the Stomach, and frequent *Singultus*, with which the Patient is continually opprefs'd. And we all know by how neceffary a kind of *Mechanifm* we do fly from and abhor thofe things which have proved dif-agreeable to the *Animal Œconomy*, to which nothing is fo contrary and repug-nant as *Pain* ; at the firft Approaches of which, Nature Starts and Recoils, tho' Reafon be arm'd with never fo much Courage and Refolution to undergo the Shock.

Nor will any Body wonder how this *Ferment* fhould caufe fuch *Torment*, who confiders how often, even in *Colical* Cafes,

Perfons

Perſons are downright diſtracted by exceſſive Pain, from a Cauſe not unlike to this we are treating of, that is, from a corroſive Ferment in the Bowels, rarefying the Juices there into *Flatus*, and by this means irritating and ſtimulating thoſe tender Membranes into Spaſmodic and Convulſive Motions.

And indeed Dr. *Liſter*'s Patient told him, that the very ſwallowing of his own Spittle put him to ſuch Torture in his Stomach, that Death it ſelf was not ſo Terrible as the Inexpreſſible Agony.

It may ſerve both to Illuſtrate and Confirm this Theory, to take Notice, that not only may (according to theſe Principles) other Bites beſides that of a *Dog* happen to induce the like Symptoms ; thus *Malpighi* (*a*) relates a Story of a Mother made *Hydrophoba* by the Bite of her *Epileptic* Daughter ; but that there are other Caſes, without any Bite at all, which are attended with an *Hydrophobia*.

Thus *Schenkius* (*b*), *Salmuth* (*c*) and others have obſerv'd a *Dread of Water*, without any Suſpicion of a Bite, from *Ma-*

(*a*) *Oper. Poſthum.* p. 55.
(*b*) *Obſer. de Venen. Animal.*
(*c*) *Obſer.* Cent. 2, Obſ. 52.

ſignant

lignant *Fevers.* Now in *These* there is
doubtless a Hot, Putrid *Ferment* in the
Blood ; and it is no wonder if Part of it
be discharged upon the Throat and Stomach, which we do evidently find in
these Distempers to be more particularly
affected by It, especially towards the latter End, from the *Aphthæ, Singultus*, and
the like usual Symptoms of a fatal Malignity.

Nay, *Hippocrates (d)* himself seems
more than once to have remarked something like this Symptom in Fevers, and
to call those who were thus affected
Βραχυπόται, or little Drinkers ; for I cannot assent to Dr. *Lister*, (tho' *Cælius Aurelianus* be on his side) who thinks that
the Βραχυπόται are ὑδροφόβοι, from the Bite
of a Mad Dog ; as well for other
Reasons, as because *Plutarch (e)* assures
Us, that the *Hydrophobia* and *Elephantiasis*
were both first taken Notice of in the
time of of *Asclepiades* the Physician ; who
liv'd in the Days of *Pompey* the Great,
many Years later than either *Hippocrates*
or *Aristotle.*

(d) *In Prorrhetic. & coac. & alibi.*
(e) *Symposiac.* 5. 9.

Nei-

Neither is it amiſs to add, that *Joannes Faber* (*f*) in the Diſſection of one who dy'd at *Rome* of the Bite of a Mad Dog, and a *Hydrophobia* ſucceeding it, found the Blood *Coagulated* in the right Ventricle of the Heart, the Lungs wonderfully *Red* and *Tumefied* ; but eſpecially the *Throat, Stomach,* and *Bowels,* bearing the Marks of the Inflammatory Venom.

The ſame Obſervation has been made by others in Bodies Dead of this Diſeaſe. Thus the *Acta Medica Hafnienſia* (*a*) relate one Caſe, in which, part of the Liver was *Inflamed ,* the Lungs Parched and Dry, and the inner Coat of the *Stomach* ſo *Mortified,* that it might be abraded with one's Fingers.

Bonetus (*b*) tells *another,* where all the *Viſcera* were found quite *arid,* without any Juice at all.

And in a very particular Hiſtory of an *Hydrophobia,* lately publiſhed at *Ulm,* (*c*) We are informed, that the *Stomach,* when opened, diſcover'd the Marks of an *Eroſion* or Excoriation, with ſomething

---

(*f*) *Apud Hernand. & Receb. Plantar. & Anim. Mexicanor. Hiſtor.* p. 494.
(*a*) Vol. 5. Obſ. 114.
(*b*) *Sepulcret.* Lib. 1. Sect. 8. Obſ. 8.
(*c*) *Roſſini Lentilii Diſſertatio de Hydrophobiæ Cauſa & Cura.*

like a Gangrene, and Suffufion of Blood here and there.   Which does very well agree with the Obfervations in the *German Ephemerides* (*d*), where we find feveral *Footfteps* of a *Sphacelus* or Mortification in the Bodies of Thofe who died *Hydrophobi.*

The Cure of this Poifon is either immediately upon the Wound made, or fome Days after, before the Fear of Water is difcover'd ; for at that time all Authors do agree the Malady to be Incurable ; and the Reafon is plain from what has been already deliver'd.

As in other Venomous Bites, fo in this, *Galen* (*e*) very wifely advifes to inlarge the Wound, by making a round Incifion about it, to Cauterife it with a hot Iron, and apply drawing Medicines, fo as to keep it a running Ulcer at leaft Forty Days. (*f*) *Scarifying* and *Cupping* may anfwer where this Severity is not allow'd :   And however, the Dreffing it with *Unguentum Ægyptiacum* (or the like) Scalding Hot, muft not be omitted ; by which alone, timely applied, I am af-

(*d*) *Eph. Cur.* Dec. 3. Ann. 2. Obf. 104.
(*e*) *De Theriac. ad Pifon.* l. 1. c. 16.
(*f*) *Vid. Aetium.* l. 6. c. 24.

fured

fured that one Bitten was happily pre-ferved.

But where thefe Means of deftroying the Ferment in the beginning are omitted, the dangerous Confequences of its being mixed with the Blood is by all poffible Care to be prevented.

To this purpofe, to fay nothing of the many Inconfiderate Jumbles of *Antidotes, Theriacas,* &c. nor of fuch vulgar Trifles as the *Liver* of the Mad Dog, of which *Galen* (a) obferved, that tho' fome who made ufe of it, together with other good Medicines, recover'd, yet that they who trufted to it alone died ; one of the greateft Remedies commended to us by Antiquity, is the *Cineres Cancrorum Fluviatilium* ; which *Galen* (b) fays, no Body ever made ufe of, and mifcarried ; and before Him *Diofcorides* (c) affured, that 'tis a Medicine may be rely'd on. Thefe were given in large Quantities, *viz.* a good Spoonful or Two every Day for Forty Days together, either alone, or rather mix'd with the Powder of *Gentian Root* and *Frankincenfe.* The *Vehicle* was either Water or Wine. In like man-

(a) *Simpl. Medic. Facult.* l. 11. c. 1.
(b) *Ibid.* l. 111. c. 34.
(c) *Theriac.* Cap. 2.

ner

ner at this Day the Remedy in the greateſt Repute of any againſt moſt Poiſons in the *Weſt-Indies*, is a kind of a *River-Craw-Fiſh*, call'd *Aratu* (d).

This is manifeſtly an *Abſorbent*, and very *Diuretic* Medicine, eſpecially when prepared after the right manner, which was by Burning the Craw-Fiſh alive upon a *Copper-Plate*, with a Fire made of the Cuttings or Twigs of *White Briony* : For whether the latter part of the Management ſignifies much or no, the former moſt certainly does ; and the *Salt* of the *Copper*, which powerfully provokes Urine, being mix'd with that of the *Aſhes*, may very much exalt their Virtue.

And it is upon this ſame Score, that the *Spongia* of the *Cynorrhodos* or *Roſa Sylveſtris* is ſo Celebrated an Antidote, not only for this Poiſon, but alſo for that of the Viper, *Tarantula*, and others too, that 'tis call'd in *Sicily Sanatodos*, or All-heal ; this being not a *Vegetable*, as P. *Boccone* (e), who has wrote a whole Letter of its wondrous Virtues, terms it, but an *Animal Alkali*, as well as the former ; for as Mr. *Ray* (f) has obſerved,

(d) *Vid. Piſon. Hiſtor. Nat. & Med. Ind.* lib. 5. c. 16.
(e) *Muſeo di Piante rare*, Oſſervaz. 2.
(f) *Hiſt. Plant. Tom.* 2. p. 1471.

this

this Spongy Excrefcence, if it be cut, is found full of White Worms ; Being the Neft of thefe Infects, which lodging here all the Winter, do in the beginning of the Spring turn to Flies, and quit their Quarters. Indeed this Remedy was antiently too of fo great Efteem, that *Pliny* recommends it as the only Cure of an *Hydrophobia*, divinely difcovered by an Oracle *(g)*.

As all Infects abound with a Diuretick Salt, fo *Cantharides* more than any others ; therefore the Learned *Bacchius* *(h)* goes farther , and from the Authority of *Rhazes* and *Joannes Damafcenus*, advifes to give thefe in Subftance for many Days together. The Preparation of this Antidote, (fo he calls it) is by infufing the *Cantharides* in Soure Butter-milk Twenty Four Hours, then drying them, and with the Flower of Lentils and Wine making them up into *Troches* of a Scruple Weight, of which one is to be taken every Day. By which means he affures us, that tho. the Patient make bloody Urine, yet that Milk largely drank will abate that Symptom, and that an *Hydrophobia* will be hap-

(f) Hiftor. Plant. Tom. 2. pag. 1471.
(g) Hiftor. Natur. l. 8. c. 41. & l. 25. cap. 2.
(h) De Venen. p. 80.

H   pily

pily prevented.   *Boccone* (*i*) tells Us,
That in *Upper Hungary* They give *Cantharides* to Men bitten by a Mad Dog, *Five*
to a Dose; and to *Beasts* in greater Quantity.   But of the inward Use of these Flies
more in its proper Place.

In short, all the *Specifics* in this Case
are such as do either absorb a peccant
Acidity in the Stomach, or carry it off by
Urine; as *Terra Lemnia*, highly commended by *Galen* (*k*), *Garlick*, *Agrimony*,
Oxylapathum, and many others, of which
a Catalogue may be seen in *S. Ardoynus*. So
the *Alyssum* or Madwort, celebrated for this
use by the Ancient Physicians, as well *that*
described by *Diascorides*, which is a Species of *Leucoium*, as the other of *Galen*,
which is a *Marrubium*, is very manifestly
a Bitter, Stomachic, and Diuretic Plant
(*l*).   The *Lichen cinereus terrestris*, recommended in the Philosophical Trans-
actions (*m*), Operates the same way.

But the greatest and surest Cure of all,
is frequent *Submerging* or Ducking the

(*i*) *Museo di Fisica*, Osservaz. 21.
(*k*) *Medicam. facult.* lib. 9. c. 1.
(*l*) *Fab. column. Phytobasan.* pag. 27.
(*m*) *No.* 237.

Patient

Patient in Water. The firſt mention I find of this is in *Cornelius Celſus* (*n*) ; whether he had it from the Ancient *Grecian* Phyſicians, or it was the Diſcovery of his own Age, matters but little to our Purpoſe ; certain it is, that he collected his Principal Rules of Bathing from *Cleophantus*, who, as *Pliny* ſays (*o*), did, beſides many other delightful things, firſt introduce the Uſe of Baths ; As appears by comparing the Writings of the *One* with the Fragments of the *Other*, preſerv'd in the Works of *Galen*. And that from *Aſclepiades*, who afterwards ſo far improved this Part of Phyſick, that he diſcarded almoſt all inward Medicines, he might learn this Management, is not improbable ; for the *Hydrophobia* (as we before took Notice) having been firſt regarded in the time of this great Phyſician, 'tis very likely that among other Advantages of his new Method, he might commend it for the Cure of ſo deplorable a Malady.

However it be, This Practice was in this laſt Age with great Authority revived

(*n*) *Lib.* 5. c. 27.
(*o*) *Nat. Hiſt.* l. 26. c. 3.

by

by the Ingenious *Baron Van Helmont* (*a*), who having in his own Country feen how great Service it did, has at large fet down both the manner of the Operation; and, Confonant to the Principles of his own Philofophy, fhewn the Reafon of its good Effects. Since him *Tulpius* (*b*), an Obferver of very good Credit, takes notice, that tho' he faw many, yet that never one mifcarry'd, where it was in time made ufe of.

As all Baths do chiefly act by the fenfible Qualities of Heat and Cold, and the Gravity of their Fluid; fo we need go no farther to fetch the Reafon of the great Advantage of this Method in the prefent Cafe, than to the Preffure of the Water upon the Body of the Patient.

Every one knows how plentifully plunging into cold Water provokes Urine, which proceeds no doubt from the conftriction hereby made of the Fibres of the Skin and Veffels. Thus this outward Cure differs not much in effect from the inward Medicines beforementioned, but muft neceffarily have the better of them in this Refpect, that when the Ferment-

(*a*) *Tr. Demens* Idea.
(*b*) Obferv. 20.

ing

ing Blood ftretches its Veffels, the exceed-
ing weight of the ambient Fluid refifts
and repreffes this Diftenfion, and fo pre-
vents the Effects of It. For this Reafon
the Salt Water of the Sea is efpecially
chofen for this Bufinefs, becaufe its greater
Gravity than that of Frefh does more
powerfully do all this, and break the beginning Cohæfion of the Parts of the
Blood.

Thus we may, without having recourfe
to the *Fright* and *Terror*, with which
this Method, when rightly practis'd, (by
keeping the Party under Water for a confiderable time, till he is almoft quite
drowned) is ufually accompanied, probably enough account for the Advantages
of this Immerfion. Tho' it is not unlike-
ly that this new Fear may have fome
good Effect in the Cafe too, for not only
Convulfions, but Agues, and other Difeafes, have oftentimes been happily Cured,
merely by terrifying and furprifing the
Patient.

The Reafon of this will eafily be underftood by him who knows what Alterations the Paffions of the Mind do make
in the Fluid of the Nerves and Arteries;
of which in another Place

It may for our prefent purpofe fuffice
to take Notice, That as in Confideration
of the laſt mentioned Effect upon the
Mind, *Van Helmont* commends this fame
Practice in all Sorts of Madneſs, and
Chronical *Deliria*; fo upon the account
of the before hinted Alterations on the
Body, Bathing was, among the Ancients,
the common Cure of Melancholy, and fuch
like Diſtempers (*c*). And as the younger
Van Helmont (*d*), to confirm his Father's
Notions, tells Us, that one Dr. *Richard-
ſon* did with wonderful Succeſs make uſe
of this Management in theſe Caſes, fo in
like manner *Proſper Alpinus* (*e*) takes Notice, that the *Egyptians* do at this Day
perfectly recover Melancholy Perſons by
the fame Method, only with this Difference, that they make their Baths warm.

He that compares what has been alrea-
dy advanc'd concerning *Deliria*, with the
Bellinian Theory of Melancholy and Ma-
niacal Diſtempers, and reflects upon the
Nature of Baths, and their manner of
Acting, will fee fo much Reafon in this
Practice, as to be forry that 'tis now-a-

(c) Vid. *Aretæum Cappad. Cur. Diut.* lib. 1. cap. 5. Et
   Aetium, l. 6. c. 11.
(d) Tr. Man and his Difeaſes.
(e) *Medicin. Ægyptior.* l. 3. c. 19.

days

days almoft quite laid afide and neglected.
For we muft obferve, that altho' there be
fome Difference in the Treatment and
Cure of *Deliria*, whether Maniacal or
Melancholy, when they are Originally
from the Mind, as the Effects of Care,
Trouble, or the like, and when from an
Indifpofition of the Body ; yet that both
do agree in this, that they require an Alteration to be made in the Blood and Spirits ; inafmuch as the Mind, by often,
nay, almoft continually, renewing *to* it
felf any one *Idea*, of Love, Sorrow, *&c.*
does fo conftantly determine the Spirits
and Blood, one and the fame way, that
the Body does at laft as much fhare in the
Alteration, as if it had been primarily affected, and confequently muft have, in
fome manner, the fame Amendment. Upon this Score *Baccius (f)* afferts the admirable Ufe of Temperate Baths, in all
kind of Diftractions; and affures us, that
not only common *Deliria*, but even the
Dæmoniaci, Phanatici, Lycanthropi themfelves, *&c.* are cured by frequent Wafh-
ings in frefh Water, and a moift and
Nourifhing Diet.

(f) De Therm. *l. 7. c.* 22.

But

But to infift upon this Subject is foreign to our purpofe; only in regard that the moft ufual Methods of Cure in thefe Cafes are fo very tedious, and oftentimes unfuccefsful at the laft, I thought it not amifs to hint thus much, in order to the advancing fomething more Certain and Effectual towards the Removal of the greateft Unhappinefs to which Mankind is liable.

To conclude with the *Hydrophobia*; where thefe Remedies fail, or are Adminiftred too late, the Patient, from the prevailing inflammatory Difpofition of the Blood, grows more and more *Delirous*, and by Degrees downright raving Mad, at laft (as it moft commonly happens in Maniacal People) fuffers a total Refolution of Strength, and Dies. Thus Dr. *Howna's* Cafe ended in a perfect univerfal *Paralyfis.*

ESSAY

ESSAY III.

OF

Poifonous Minerals

AND

PLANTS.

ALtho' there be a great Variety of Internal *Poifons*, as well *Mineral* as *Vegetable*; yet they do all of 'em feem to agree in their Primary Effects, and Manner of Operation; and as the Teeth or Stings of *Venomous* Animals do conftantly infufe a Juice into the Wound they make, by which the Mafs of Blood is infected; fo the Force of *Thefe* is chiefly confined to the Stomach and

Primæ

Primæ Viæ ; and tho' it may in some Cases be Comunicated Farther, yet the Principal Mischief is done in These Parts.

Deleterious Medicines, says Dioscorides, *are many, but the Alterations made by them in the Body, common, and but few (a)*.

Of all this kind, those of a *Mineral* Nature are the most violent and deadly, the greater Gravity and Solidity of their Parts giving to these a Force and Action surpassing the mischief of *Vegetable* Juices ; and therefore whereas noxious Plants do vary their Effects in different Creatures, so as to prove harmless, nay, perhaps Beneficial and Nutritive to some, as Hemlock they say is to Goats (b) and Starlings (c), and Henbane to Hogs (d), the Strength of the Stomach in These Animals being sufficient to Conquer and Divide such Corrosive Substances, and their Blood perhaps requiring to be recruited by such warm and active Particles; A Mineral Malignity is not, at least so far

---

(a) Ποικίλα μὲν γὰρ τὰ δηλητήσια φάρμακα, κοιναὶ δὲ κỳ ὀ πολλαὶ ἐξ αὐτῶν γινόμϸαι διαθέσεις. *Alexiph.* pag. 399.

(b) *Lucret.* lib. 5.

(c) *Galen. Simp. Medic.* l. 3. cap. 18.

(d) *Sext. Empiric. Hypoth. Empiric.* 1.

as we know, conquerable by any, but becomes univerfally hurtful and deftructive.

We fhall here give the firft Place to *Mercury Sublimate*.

This is no other than a Mixture of *Quickfilver* with *common Salt*. The way of preparing it, as 'tis made at *Venice*, from whence great quantities are fent into other Countries, *Tachenius* has given Us in his *Hippocrates Chymicus* (e); as to which we muft obferve, that tho' there be always added a proportion of *Salt-Petre*, and *Calcin'd Vitriol* to the other Ingredients, yet thefe do not enter into the Compofition, but only ferve to facilitate the Work ; as abundantly appears from this Experiment, That Mercury fublim'd with the fame Proportion of Nitre and Vitriol without *Marine Salt*, neither receives any increafe of its Weight, nor acquires any malignant Quality.

The Effects of this *Poifon* when taken are, violent Griping Pains, with a Diftenfion of the Belly, Vomiting of a flimy, frothy Matter, fometimes mixt with Blood, and Stools of the fame, an intolerable Heat and Thirft, with cold Sweats,

---

(e) *Cap.* 24.

Tremblings,

Tremblings, Convulsions, *&c.* as will appear from the following History (*f*).

To a large Dog was given a Drachm of *Mercury Sublimate*, mixt with a little Bread ; within a quarter of an Hour He fell into terrible Vomitings, casting up frequently a Viscid, frothy *Mucus*, every time more and more Bloody, and purged the same downwards ; till tired and spent with this hard Service, He lay down quietly as it were to Sleep, but Died the next Morning.

The *Abdomen* being opened, a great quantity of extravasated Blood was found between the Liver and Stomach, and between the duplicature of the *Omentum* about the Stomach ; the Guts as well as the Stomach were distended, and full of a frothy Bloody *Mucus* ; on the outside they were of a livid Colour, within all over red, and inflamed down to the very *Rectum* ; The Fibrous Coat of the Stomach being taken off, between that and the Nervous one, grumous Blood was found in several Places ; the like was discovered here and there in the Intestins between the same Coats.

(*f*) *Wepfer de Cicut. Aquatic.* pag. 300.

The

The ſame *Symptoms* with theſe, and ma-nifeſt Signs of a burning Corroſion follow-ed with *Ulcers* in the Bowels, *Baccius* (g) obſerv'd in a young Man Poiſon'd by *Sub-limate,* mixt with his Meat.

What we are here chiefly to examine is, how from Ingredients ſingly Innocent and Harmleſs, ſo Miſchievous a Compound can reſult ; for as the Caſe is very plain with reſpect to *Salt,* ſo is it likewiſe now No-torious enough, that *Quick-ſilver* it ſelf, which the Ancients, *Dioſcorides, Galen, Pliny,* &c. have unjuſtly rank'd among Poiſons, is in many Diſeaſes inwardly ta-ken of very ſafe and beneficial Uſe ; and that not only when diſguiſed with *Sul-phur, Sugar,* &c. but *Crude,* without any Correction, or vainly pretended Mortifi-cation.

This the *Arabian* Phyſicians firſt gave the hint of; *Avicen,* (h) having obſerv'd, that *They who drink It in a large quan-tity receive no hurt, its weight making a free Paſſage thro' the Body.* This was In-couragement enough for the Practice of giving whole Pounds of It in the *Iliac*

g) *De Venen.* pag. 21.
h) *Can. Medic.* l. 4. Fen. 6. *Argentum Vivum plurimum qui bibunt non læduntur eo; egreditur enim cum diſſoſi-tione ſuâ per inferiorem regionem.*

Paſſion;

Paſſion ; which is oftentimes done with good Succeſs, without any frightful Symptom accompanying the Advantage receiv'd from its Ponderoſity.

Afterwards it plainly appear'd that this Mineral, tho' not taken in ſo great a Doſe as could immediately force its way thro' the Inteſtins, even when it was lodged for ſome time in this or that Part, was not at all hurtful by any Corroſive or Malignant Quality. And *Fallopius* (i), *Braſavolus* (k), with others of great Note, confirmed its harmleſs Efficacy in the Cure of the *Worms*, not only in adult Perſons, but even in the more tender Conſtitutions of Children.

Nor are theſe the only Caſes in which good Service may be had from this Weighty Fluid ; he that rightly conſiders the State of the Animal *Oeconomy*, the various Alterations it ſuffers from the Stagnation of its more Viſcid Juices in the ſmalleſt Canals, and how much the Impulſe and Force of the Circling Blood, by which Obſtructions are to be removed, muſt be increaſed by its carrying along with it ſuch Particles as the

(i) *De Morb. Gallic. cap.* 76.
(k) *De Morb. Gall. inter Autores de Morb. Gall.* pag. 599.

Mercurial

Mercurial Globuli, will perhaps see good Reason to allow, that the prudent and cautious Management of *Quicksilver* may do that in some obstinate and dangerous Diseases, which we cannot promise our selves from any other of our known Medicines whatsoever.

But I am not to insist on this Head; and the learned *Author* of the *New Theory of Fevers* (*l*), has already most ingeniously explain'd the *Mechanism* by which such Effects as these are produced in the humane Body. It suffices to my present purpose, to have proved that pure *Mercury* is not Poisonous or Corrosive; and therefore not only have I seen Two Ounces of It given every Day for One and Twenty Days together, without any Inconvenience at all; but found once some quantity of It in the *Perinæum* of a Subject I took from the Gallows for a Dissection (whose rotten Bones quickly discovered what Disease it was had required the Use of it, and that I suppose chiefly in External Application by Unction) without any Marks of Corrosion of the Part where it was lodged.

(*l*) Pag. 51. & *seq.*

Tho'

Tho' withal we may upon this Occasion remark, that the extreme Gravity of this Mineral alone, however serviceable it may be in other Respects; yet when it happens in so great a Quantity to Obstruct the Capillary Ducts, as that the Force of the Circling Fluid is not sufficient to Wash it away, must necessarily induce Symptoms troublesome and bad enough, as *Spasms, Contractions, Palsies,* &c. which They do commonly Experience, who have either been too often dawbed with *Mercurial Ointments,* or for a long time imploy'd in rubbing the *Quicksilver* upon *Looking-Glasses* ; for the Internal Use of It will never produce any such Mischiefs.

As for *Sublimate* then, most certain it is, that the *Saline* Particles do impart to the *Mercury* this Malignant Quality; or to speak more properly, That the *Salt* receives from the *Mercurial Corpuscles* such an Increase of its Gravity and *Momentum,* as renders its Cutting Corrosion more Effectual and Penetrating ; for the manner after which this Matter is done, is plainly this.

The *Globules* of the *Mercury,* tho' so minutely divided by the Action of the Fire, as to rise in the form of a *Fume,*

yet

yet are still Solid and Ponderous Bodies; 'tis all one to the present purpose, whether We suppose 'em perfectly *Spherical*, or with the Learned *Gulielmini* (*a*) *Sphæroidical*, for in both Cases, by reason of their extreme Parvity, being perhaps Simple and Elementary Bodies, they will easily be lodg'd in the Pores and Interstices of the *Saline Crystals*; which being compos'd of the *Atoms* of *Salt*, variously by *Sublimation* combin'd and united, are a kind of Cutting *Lamellæ* or Blades; the force of which could never have been very penetrating, upon the account of their Lightness and easie Dissolution, if the *Mercury*, without blunting their Edge, or breaking their Figure, did not lend 'em an Additional Weight, and thus at the same time strengthen their Action, and prevent their quick Solution by the Juices of the Stomach; which cannot now disjoin their Compounding Parts, because the Vacuities into which they should, in order to do this, insinuate themselves, are already possess'd, and taken up by the *Mercurial Globules.*

In short, These *Crystals*, which are to be considered as so many sharp Knives or

---

(*a*) *Trattato de Fiumi.* Cap. 1.

I

Daggers,

Daggers, Wounding and Stabbing the tender Coats of the Stomach, and thus caufing exceffive Pains, with an Abrafion of their Natural *Mucus,* and (upon the conftant Senfe of Irritation) continual Vomitings, *&c.* muft of neceffity, fticking here and there in the capillary Veffels, ftop the Paffage of the Blood in feveral Places, whereupon it Stagnates, and there follow little Inflammations, which growing higher and higher, terminate quickly in perfect Ulcers and Gangrenes; and thefe though fingly very fmall, yet many in number, do all together make up one continued and incurable Mortification.

This being the Nature of *Sublim'd Mercury,* it may not be amifs to enquire, how it comes to pafs, That This fame Compound refublim'd with *live Mercury* in the Proportion of Four Parts to Three, (for the *Sublimate* will not take up an equal quantity) efpecially if the work be repeated Three or Four times, loofes its Corrofivenefs to that Degree as to become not only a Safe, but in many Cafes, a Noble *Medicine.* For I do not fee that any of the Chymical Writers have hit upon the true Solution of this *Phænomenon.*

Here

Here then it is to be confidered, That the Action of the *Saline Cryftals* depending upon their Solidity and Largenefs, thefe muft neceffarily, by every fubfequent Sublimation, be broken into fmaller and fmaller Parts; the *Mercurial Globules* (for the Reafons given by the *Author (a)* of the forementioned *Theory of Fevers*) arifing more quickly and eafily than the *Salts*, quit the Interftices in which they were lodged, and the *Cryftalline* Blades are divided every time more and more by the force of the Fire; whereupon a new Combination of Parts fucceeds; and although there be a greater Proportion of the *Mineral* to the *Salts* than before, which makes *Dulcify'd Mercury* Specifically heavier than the *Corrofive*; yet the broken pieces of the *Cryftals* uniting into little Maffes of differing Figures from their former Make, thofe Cutting *Points* which were before fo fharp, are now either quite loft, or at leaft, by reafon of their Bluntnefs, cannot make Wounds deep enough to be equally mifchievous and deadly; and therefore do only Vellicate and Twitch the fenfible Membranes of the Stomach to that Degree, as ex-

(*a*) Pag. 93.

I 2   cites

cites them to an Excretion of their Contents and Glandular Juices, upwards or downwards, according as the force of Irritation is greater or less.

Thus a violent *Poison* is mitigated into a *Vomit* or *Purge*; nay, it may easily happen (especially in Robust Constitutions, and if the Bowels be at the same time by any means defended against the Stimulating Power of the Medicine) that this Twitching may be so slight, as to be almost insensible, and hardly troublesome; and then the *Mercurial Globules* being freed indeed from most of the *Saline Parts* in their Passage thro' the *Prima Viæ*, but still having a mixture of some few of them, are quickly conveyed into the Blood, where by their Motion and Weight they must necessarily dissolve the Preternatural Cohæsions of all the Liquors, particularly of Those which Circulate in the smallest Canals, and are most Viscid and Tenacious, making 'em more Fluxile and Thin, or of more easie Secretion; whereupon all the Glands of the Body are, as it were, set to Work, and Scoured of their Contents; but the *Salival* Ones especially, being many in Number, very large and wide, and the Juice they separate of a Tough and Ropy Sub-

Subftance, fo that a confiderable quantity of It is accumulated before it is forced out at the Orifices of the Ducts, Thefe Effects will be moft remarkable in *Them*, and a *Salivation* or Spitting muft continue fo long, till the Active Mineral Particles are thro' thefe and the other Paffages difcharged out of the Body.

As the Difference between Mercury *Corrofive* and *Dulcified* lies in a greater and leffer Degree of Operation and Force, fo this fame Confideration diftinguifhes the feveral *Preparations* of this Mineral from each other ; which tho' very many, yet do all vary their Effects in the Body, only according as the *Mercurial Globules* are differently combined with *Salts*, and the *Points* of *Thefe* more or lefs broken by the Action of the Fire, in the Burning of Spirits upon Them, and fuch like Managements: And therefore however dignified with the great Names of *Arcana*, *Panacæa*, *Princes Powders*, &c. They do not afford Us any thing Singular and Extraordinary, beyond what we may with equal Advantage promife our felves from fome or other of the moft common and ufual *Proceffes*.

We

We may also fairly conclude from this Reasoning, that the safest way of raising a *Salivation* is by *Internal* Medicines; since whatever Mischiefs can be apprehended from *These*, may in a greater degree follow from the *External* Use of *Mercury*; not only because, as We have already hinted, the Mineral *Globules* being intimately combined with Salts in the several Preparations given inwardly, will by the Irritation of These, be easily and fully thrown out at the Organs of Secretions, till the Blood is quite discharged of its Load; whereas, in all the Dawbings with Mercurial Ointments, We can never be certain that none of the heavy Particles are left lodg'd in the *Interstices* of the *Fibres* or *Cells* of the *Bones*; But also, in as much as by computing the Portion of *Mercury* in all the Doses necessarily to promote a Spitting, and the Weight of the same Mineral usually apply'd when this is done by Unction, it will appear, that the quantity in the latter Case vastly exceeds that in the former, and consequently that the Inconveniencies to be feared will be in the same proportion.

Therefore this External Management of *Mercury* is only to be allow'd of, where either the Case will bear the Violence of
such

such a Method, or outward *Ulcers* and *Tumors* require a particular Cure by *Liniments,* &c.

Nor is it improper to Remark that, We do hereby see how the Use of this Mineral comes to produce that Effect so often complain'd of, (tho' not always with Reason) of making the Bones Foul or Carious. For, if the *Laminæ* or *Fibres* of These are already so much broken and spoiled by a Disease, as that the Circulation of the Fluids thro' 'em can't be maintain'd, they must necessarily be corrupted more by the Weight of the *Mercurial Globules*; tho' here also it is plain, that the *outward* Use of this Remedy will be more to be blamed than the *inward.*

And indeed, as the earliest Use of *Mercury* was in *Unguents* and *Emplasters,* so most of the Prejudices and Out-cries against It are owing to Effects produced this way. For the first attempts of the Cure of *Venereal Maladies* by this Remedy, were learned from the *Arabians* (a), who having recommended *Mercurial* Ointments in the *Lepra* or *Scabies,* gave a handle to the *Italian* Physicians to try their

(a) *Vid. Jaan. Baptist. Montan. Tract. de Morb. Gallic. inter Autor. de Morb. Gall. p. m.* 482. *Et Fallop. de Morb. Gall. Cap,* 76.

I 4 Efficacy,

Efficacy, in removing the Foulneſs of the Skin from a new and terrible Contagion ; neither were they ſparing of their Liniments, which they continued to rub in for 12, 15, nay, ſometimes for above 30 Days together (*b*). So that it is no wonder if they often met with very untoward Symptoms from ſo ſevere a Treament, and if, (as ſome of them (*c*) do affirm) they now and then found *Mercury* in the rotten Bones of their Patients, who had, it may be, ſuffered too much both from their Diſeaſe and their Phyſician.

Thus much of *Mercury.* Let Us in the next place examine *Arſenick,* about the Nature and Compoſition of which Authors are very much puzzled.

This, in ſhort, is either *Native* or *Factitious,* and each of Three ſorts, *Yellow, Red,* and *White.* The *Native Yellow* is what the *Latins* call'd *Auripigmentum* ;

(*b*) *Nicol. Maſs. de Morb. Gall. Tract.* 4. *Cap.* 2.

(*c*) *Argentum vivum accepi ex Oſſe Cujuſdam corrupto, quem perunctum ab Empyricis plus decies ferebant, non ſemel emanaviſſe.* Anton. Gall. *in* Lib. de Ligno Sancto non permiſcendo.

Non ſemel in Sepulcbris Argentum Vivum in Mortuorum Capitibus reperi. Anton. Muſa Braſavolus *in* Tract. de Morb. Gallic.

and

and this *Olaus Wormius (b)* makes Three-fold. The *Red* is the *Sandaracha* of the *Greeks.* The *White* was not known to the Ancients ; and indeed *Theophrastus* seems only to have known the *Red* ; but *Dioscorides* describes both *Red* and *Yellow* ; *Nicander* had no Knowledge of either ; The only Mineral Poisons He mentions are *Litharge* and *Ceruss.*

Orpiment and *Sandaracha* differ only by their greater or lesser Concoction in the Earth ; and therefore from *Orpiment* Boiled in a close Pot Five Hours in a Furnace Fire, is made the *Factitious Sandaracha,* as perfect as the *Natural (c).*

The *Factitious Yellow* is made from the Crusts of the *Natural Orpiment (d).*

The *Native White* is more rare, but found plentifully in some Silver Mines in *Germany (e).*

But the *White Factitious* is of the most common Use of all ; and it is, as *Agricola* tells us, no other than *Orpiment* again and again sublimed with an equal part of *Fossile Salt,* till it is brought to a Whiteness.

(b) *Museum,* p. 28.
(c) *Agricola de Natura Fossil.* p. m. 592.
(d) *Idem, Ibid.*
(e) *Block Scrutinum Arsenici,* §. XIV.

Orpiment

Orpiment and *Sandaracha* are moſtly
found in Mines of God ; and all Metallic Writers do agree them to be the
beſt Signs of the Richneſs of the Vein.
This is Ground ſufficient for the *Chymiſts*
to take *Arſenick* for the Subject Matter
of their great Work, as they call It ; and
they have very fondly accommodated
ſome Ænigmatical Lines in the *Sibylline
Oracles* (*f*) to this *Mineral.* Tho' the
Interpretation be ſtrained, and not fairly
made out, (the *Author* of theſe Verſes,
whatever he might mean, being indeed
Diſcourſing of the Name of the *Divine
Power* it ſelf) yet very true it is, that
this great Expectation from *Arſenick* is as
old at leaſt as *Caligula* ; that is, of more
ancient Date conſiderably than the far
greateſt part of thoſe Suppoſitious and
Ill-contrived Compoſitions which do now
bear the Name of *Oracles* : For that Co-
vetous Emperor, as *Pliny* relates (*g*), ordered a great quantity of *Orpiment* to be
wrought upon, that He might extract

(f) *Lib.* 1.
Ἐννέα γράμματ' ἔχω, τετρασυλλαβός εἰμι, νόει με.
Αἱ τρεῖς αἱ πρῶται δύο γράμματ' ἔχουσιν ἑκάςη,
Ἡ λοιπὴ δὲ τὰ λοιπὰ, ᾗ εἰσὶν ἄφωνα τὰ πέντε.
Τῦ παντὸς δ' ἀριθμῦ ἑκατον[άδες εἰσὶ δὶς ὀκτω,
Καὶ τρεῖς τρὶς δεκάδες.
(g) Nat. Hiſt. *l.* 33. *c.* 4.

Gold

Gold out of It, and made some ; but as it usually happens in such like Attempts, the quantity did not answer the Expence.

It is more to our purpose to take notice, that the later *Pretenders* to this *Philosophy*, by finding their three *Principles, Salt, Sulphur*, and *Mercury* in this Body, will lead Us into its true Nature and Composition.

For whether We take *Orpiment* or *Sandaracha*, either of them will afford a *Regulus* or Mercurial Substance, more pure than that of *Antimony*. The manner of extracting It *Lemery* (*h*) has taught ; and to This indeed the Mineral owes its great Ponderosity.

The Inflammability and Smell of *Arsenick* are sufficient Proofs of its abounding *Sulphur*, which may without much difficulty be separated from It (*i*).

That it consists of some *Saline Parts* we are assured by Its Solution in common Water (*k*) ; and it is upon the account of These that It does more happily promote the *Flowing* of Metals than any o-

---

(*h*) *Cours de Chymie*, Part 1. Chap. 10.
(*i*) *Lemery*, ibid.
(*k*) *Vid. Eman. Konig Regn. Mineral.* and *Boyle* History of Mineral Waters.

ther

ther *Salt-Pouders* which the Workmen make ufe of : Wherefore fome have called It a coagulated *Aqua Fortis.*

From all this it appears, that Authors do vainly Difpute wherein the Noxious quality of *Arfenick* refides, fince the Cafe here is plainly much the fame with that of *Sublimate Corrofive* ; and as the Salts there, together with the Mercurial Particles, do compofe pungent *Cryftals,* fo without all doubt the *Regulus* of this Mineral gives a like force to the *Saline Bodies,* which without this weight could be but of fmall Effect. The main difference is, that in *Arfenick* we have an addition of *Sulphur,* which does not only ftrengthen the Action of the other Parts, in that as a *Vinculum* it keeps them united together ; but confifting befides of many hot and fiery Corpufcles, promotes the Inflammation of thofe Wounds which the Cryftalline *Spicula* make in the Membranes of the Stomach.

Upon the Score of fuch a Texture and Make as this, *Arfenick* makes no Ebullition either with *Alcalies* or *Acids* (*a*) ; and *as* the *Regulus* of It being cleared from moft of its Salts, is by much lefs

_____

(a) *Grew* of Mixture, *pag. m.* 246.

hurtful

hurtful than the crude Mineral it self; so on the other Hand, the *Factitious White*, in which there is a much greater Proportion of the Saline to the Metallic Parts, is the most Violent of all the kinds, superiour in Force to *Mercury Sublimate*.

The several Histories related by *Wepfer* (*b*) do put this out of Question; It is sufficient to our Purpose to mention One.

A Dog having eat some Fat mixt with *White Arsenic*, died the next Day; The upper Part of the Stomach, when opened, was red and inflamed, the Coats thinner than ordinary, the bottom of It was covered with a fætid Slime, and some Pieces of Fat; the Thin Guts were so Corroded as to be Pervious in Three Places, Two of the Ulcers so large that they would easily admit a *Bean*. The Cavity of the *Abdomen* contained a yellowish *Ichor* tinged with Blood.

The Case being thus, one would wonder what should induce Authors to prescribe so Corrosive a Mineral to be worn upon the *Pit* of the Stomach, as an *Amulet* against the Plague. This Trick we may well believe to be Dangerous, when *Lio-*

***

(*b*) *Cicut. aquat.* pag. 274. & *seq.*

nardo di Capo (*c*) tells Us of a Child a‑
kill'd by the Violent Vomiting and Pur-
ging, occafion'd from a flight Wound
made in the Head by a *Comb* wet with
Oil in which *Arfenick* had been infufed;
for the Pores of the Body being opened
by Heat and Exercife, fome of the Noxious *Effluvia* may eafily Infinuate them-
felvs into the Part; accordingly *Crato* (*d*)
obferv'd an Ulcer of the Breaft caufed by
this Application; *Verzafcha* (*e*) Violent Pains, and fainting Fits; *Diemer-
brock* (*f*), and Dr. *Hodges* (*g*), Death it
felf.

The Truth of the Matter is, This Practice feems to owe its Origine to a Mi-
ftake (*h*), fome of the *Arabian* Phyficians
had commended *Darfini* worn in a Bag for
a Prefervative in Plague time; This in
their Language fignifies *Cinnamom*; but
the *Latin* Interpreters retaining the fame
Word in their Tranflations (as was frequently done), one or other afterwards
not underftanding its meaning, and de-

(c) *Incertezza de Medicament*, p. m. 82.
(d) *Epiftol.* 168.
(e) Obfervation 66.
(f) *De Pefte*, Hiftor. 99.
(g) *De Pefte Londinenf.* p. 239.
(h) *A. Deufingius de Pefte*, Part 4. Sect. 3. c. 3.

ceived

ceived by the likeness of the sound, sub-
stitued in its Place *De Arsenico*, as if *Dar-
sini* were all one with *Zarnich*. The Authority of the first Author served to pro-
pagate the Error ; nor were Those wanting
who reason'd upon the Matter, and found
it agreable to their Philosophy, that this
Mineral should draw to it self and con-
center the *Arsenical Effluvia* out of the
Air, and thus secure the Body from their
Infection ; These being, as they imagined, the Common Cause of Pestilential
Diseases.

Having thus particularly Discoursed
of the Nature of these Two Poisons, I
shall not need to insist upon any more
out of the *Mineral Kingdom*.

All of *Them* bear some Analogy to the
former, and are more or less Dangerous,
according as their *Salts* receive a differing
Force from the *Metallic* Particles. For
this Reason as we have observed, that
the most Virulent may be mitigated by
breaking the *Points* of the *Saline Crystals* ;
so on the other Hand, the most Innocent
Minerals may become Corrosive, by com-
bining Them with *Salts*, as we see in the
several Preparations of *Silver, Antimony,
Iron,* &c.

Poisonous

Poisonous Plants.

TO Proceed therefore to *Vegetables* ; the most Notorious of *These* for Venomous Juices among the Ancients were *Cicuta* and *Aconitum.*

Our *Œnanthe Cicutæ facie, succo viroso,* which *Wepfer* has described by the Name of *Cicuta Aquatica,* and of the dismal Effects of which in some Children, who by mistake did Eat of It, He has wrote a large Volume, was very probably the *Cicuta* so much in use of old, especially at *Athens,* for *Killing.* At least the Violence of *This* makes It a much fitter Instrument of Death than the common *Hemlock,* which is not by far of so Malignant a quality.

Tho' we must withal allow differing *Climates* very considerably to heighten or abate the *Virtues* of *Plants.* And it is not altogether Improbable, that the Poison with which the *Athenians* took away the Lives of Malefactors was an inspissated Juice compounded of *That* of *Cicuta* and other Corrosive Herbs (*i*).

(i) *Vide* Wepfer, *Pag.* 60.

But

But be this as it will ; The Alterations which *Wepfer* obferved the Roots of *Œnanthe* to make in the Body, were a Violent Pain and Heat in the Stomach, Terrible Convulfions, with the Lofs of all the Senfes, Diftorfion of the Eyes, and flowing of Blood out at the Ears, the Mouth fo faft fhut that no Art could open It, Efforts to Vomit, but nothing thrown up, frequent Hick-Coughs, with a great Diftenfion and Swelling, efpecially at the Pit of the Stomach ; and when Death had concluded the Tragedy, a continued Running of green Froth at the Mouth.

Stalpart van der Wiel gives Us the like account of Two Perfons kill'd at the *Hague* by the fame *Roots* (*k*).

In a *Dog*, who for Experiment's fake died by this *Poifon*, The Stomach when opened was found quite *Conftringed*, and fhut up at both *Orifices*, Its inward Surface red, with livid Spots here and there ; The Inteftines were empty ; only the *Rectum* contained a little greenifh *Mucus*.

Thus it appears, that this Plant confifts of Hot, Acrious and Corrofive Parts, which by Rarefying the Juices of the

(k) *Obfervat. Centur.* 1. Obf. 43.

K

Stomach.

Stomach, and Wounding Its Nervous Membrane, are the Caufe of all thofe Diforders which do immediately follow.

For upon the Senfe of a violent *Irritation* and *Pain*, the Fluid of the Nerves is prefently in large quantities determined to the Part affected ; and this, if the *Stimulus* be not over great, will be only to fuch a Degree as is fufficient, by contracting the Fibres of the Stomach, and Mufcles of the *Abdomen*, to throw off the Caufe of the *Difagreable Senfation* ; but the uneafie *Twitching* being too terrible to be born, the Mind, by a kind of furprize, does with *Hafte* and *Fury* as it were Command the Spirits thither ; Thus the Bufinefs is over-done, and the Action of the Fibres becomes fo ftrong, that the Orifices of the Stomach are quite clofed ; fo that inftead of difcharging the Noxious Matter, The *Torment* is made greater, and the whole *Œconomy* put into Confufion.

This forcible Contraction of the Mufcles was the Reafon that one of the Children which *Wepfer* faw, made *Urine* in the midft of the Agony, to the height of Five or Six Foot, with a ftrength and violence Surprifing to the Spectators.

Nor

Nor is it any wonder, if in these *Circumstances* all Sense be lost, Blood gush out at the *Ears, Nostrils,* &c. the Parts being all torn and broke by the Violence of the *Convulsions*; which tho' they began in the Muscles of the Belly, must at last prevail in the Members too, till the whole Fabrick is shock'd and overturn'd; and some of the *Corrosive Salts* perhaps getting into the Blood, and by the Rarefaction of It Distending the Vessels, The Membranous Coats of which being already overstretched, will the more easily give way, and let out their Fluid.

The Case of *Aconitum* is much the same; this is our *Napellus* or *Monkshood*; and its Effects do so nearly agree with those now related of *Œnanthe,* that I shall not need to recite Them; the Experiments of *Wepfer* (*a*) are full and convincing. And indeed *as* all the *Histories* which this same *Author* has so carefully given Us of Trials made with several Vegetable Poisons, *Solanum, Nux Vomica, Coculus Indicus,* &c. on different Creatures, do put it out of all doubt, that the common Mischief of *These* is a Twitch-

(*a*) Pag. 176. *seq.*

K 2

ing

ing and Inflammation of the Stomach; *so* it appears from hence, that *Virulent Plants*, although they may be diftinguifhed even from one another by *particular Virtues*, do however *Kill* by a like Operation and Force, which differs chiefly in Degree from *That* of Noxious Minerals.

And therefore in order to know what the *Specifick Qualities* of any fuch *Herbs* are, they muft be given only in very fmall *Dofes*; and then perhaps it would appear, that they are not made (as fome do imagine) to be Deleterious and Deftructive, but for very Good and Beneficial Ufes; as we do particularly Experience in the Cafe of *Opium.*

Nor is it at all ftrange, that the *Symptoms* from a *Vegetable*, and from a *Mineral* Virulency, fhould be fo different, although of the fame kind, and only of unequal force; for the more folid Parts of *Minerals*, eroding the Coats of the Stomach, induce a perfect Mortification and Gangrene, and thus do their Work at once; whereas the weaker Salts of *Plants* can make but a flighter *Excoriation*, upon the painful Senfe of which thofe Agonies and Convulfions that follow do rather gradually exhauft the Strength;

Strength; and thus the Animal is not kill'd so speedily, nor with the same *Appearances*.

Upon this Score, tho' Mineral Poisons do not pass the *Primæ Viæ*, Vegetable ones in some Cases possibly may; just as We find Those Medicines which have a great Degree of Irritation presently to induce a *Vomiting*; whereas the same *Twitching* a little weakened suffers them to pass into the Intestines, and *Work* downwards by Stools.

By this We may perhaps give some Guess at the Nature of those *Poisons*, with which They tell Us the *Natives* in some Parts of *Africa* and *India* are so expert at Killing, that they can do It in a longer or shorter time as they please. These are most probably either the *Fruits*, or the Inspissated *Juices* of Corrosive Plants, which inflaming the Bowels, may cause little Ulcers there, whose Fatal Consequences, we know, may very well be slow and lingering.

This I am the rather induced to believe, because an Ingenious *Surgeon*, who liv'd in *Guinea*, told Me, that the *Antidote* by which the *Negroes* would sometimes Cure Those who were *poisoned*,

K 3

was

was the *Leaf* of an *Herb* which purged both upwards and downwards. For by this means the Stomach might be cleared from the adhering Corrosive Parts of the Venom. Yet I can hardly think it possible at the same time that they should be able, by varying the Composition or Quantity of the *Dose*, to ascertain the Time in which It shall Kill, to a Week, Month, &c. nor indeed have I ever met with any Person who could Attest This, to be Matter of Fact.

Tho' repeated Trials and Observations may help one well practised in such Tricks to give notable Conjectures in this Point.

The Ancients indeed pretended much the same thing with their *Aconitum,* of which They seem to have made a kind of Secret and Mystery ; as we learn from *Theophrastus* (a), who says, *The ordering of this Poison was different, according as It was designed to Kill in Two, Three Months, or a Year :* But this he relates only as a common *Tale* or *Opinion,* and not as a Story to which Himself gave any manner of Credit.

_____

(a) *Hist. Plant.* l. 9. c. 16.

It

It is very plain; that the common *Cure* of all *Poifons* of this kind, muft be by freeing the Stomach, as foon as poflible, from the Corrofive Vellicating Particles, and defending the Membranes from their Acrimony, by fuch Things as are of a a Smooth, Oily and Lubricating Subftance.

K 4   ESSAY

ESSAY IV.

OF

OPIUM.

THE Ancients having Experienced that *Opium* would oftentimes Kill, though taken in no large quantity, ranked It with *Poisons*, and gave It the first place among Those, which from their Stupefying Quality They call'd *Narcotic*.

True indeed it is, that We do every Day find This to be, in a small Dose, one of the most Noble Remedies in the World. But it is not worth the while to engage in the Controversie warmly debated by some *Authors*, how far *Poisons* are Medicinal; since it is notorious enough, that Medicines do sometimes prove *Poisonous*. And take the Matter as We
                                    please,

pleafe, it may ferve to very good Purpofes to underftand the manner of Operation of fo Celebrated a *Drug*, and help
Us in a great Meafure to afcertain Its Ufe
in different Cafes, if we are beforehand
rightly apprifed of Its Nature and Way
of Acting.

In order hereunto, it is neceffary, befides fome other *Præcognita*, fince one of
the chief Virtues of this Medicine Is
Hypnotic, to Define diftinctly what *Sleep*
is, or rather, (to avoid Confufion and
Difputes about Words) what Difference
there is between an Animal Body when
afleep and when *awake*. For I fuppofe
the *Hiftory, Manner of Preparing,* &c.
of *Opium*, to be already fufficiently
known.

Firft then, There is no One but knows
that in *Sleep* there is a Ceffation from
Action. When *Waking*, We Walk, Difcourfe, Move this or that Limb, *&c.* but
in natural and undifturbed *Reft* there is
nothing of all Thefe; that is, whereas
being awake, We do perform feveral Motions by the *voluntary* Contraction of our
Mufcles; when afleep, thofe Mufcles only are Contracted, whofe Action is in a
manner *Involuntary*, or to which the
Mind has always fo conftantly determin'd
the

the Spirits, that It does it by a *Habit,* without the Intervention of the Reasoning Faculty; such are *Those* of the Heart and Breast.

So that there is at this time a kind of *Relaxation* or Loosness of the moving Fibres of the several Members; or at least such a quiet Position and State of them, by which all the *Antagonist* Muscles are in an *Æquilibrium* and Equality of Action, not overpowering one another. For this indeed seems to be one great Design of Sleep, to recover to the Parts overstretched by Labour their former *Tone* and Force; and therefore we do naturally, when composing our selves to *Rest,* put our Body into that Posture which does most Favour the *particularly* wearied Limbs, and conduce to this end.

In the next place, it is very plain that there is in *Sleep* not only a Rest and Suspension from Acting of most of our Bodily Organs, but even of our *Thinking Faculty* too. That is (for I would prevent Cavils) a ceasing from such *Thoughts* as when Waking We are exercised about, which we do *Reflect* upon, and *Will* to employ our Mind with. For though *Dreams* are Thoughts, yet they are but imperfect and incoherent Ones,

and

and are indeed either fo faint and languid *Reprefentations*, as to be confiftent with our *Sleep*, as fome may be; or elfe if they be ftrong and lively, they are, as every one knows, the *Interruption* and Difturbance of It.

From hence It will follow, That the *Motion* of the Arterial Fluid muft be, *Ceteris Paribus*, more fedate, even and regular, in the time of *Sleeping* than *Waking*; For, befides the various Alterations which in the latter State this receives from the feveral *Paffions* of the Mind, the very *Contractions* of the Mufcles themfelves in Exercifes of the Body do differently forward its Courfe; whereas in *Sleep* the force of the Heart and Pectoral Mufcles being more conftant and uniform, gives it a more calm and equally continued Impulfe.

Hence alfo it will come to pafs, that the *Influx* of the *Liquor* of the Nerves into the Organs of the Body, as alfo Its *Reflux* towards the *Brain*, is in Sleep either none, or very inconfiderable; that is, that this Fluid has at this time but little or no *Motion*. For 'tis Mufcular *Action* and *Senfation* that require It to be thus determin'd, this way or that, which are now hardly any. And yet by the arrival

of

of Blood at the Brain, this *Juice* will still be feparated there, fit to be derived into its Canals or Tubes. So that by this means there will be a kind of *Accumulation,* or laying up in Store, of *Spirits* for the Offices and Requirements of *Waking.*

Thus We may in fhort look upon the time of *Watching,* as the time of Wearing out, or the Deftruction of the Animal Fabrick ; and the time of *Sleep,* as that in which it is repaired and recruited ; not only upon the account of what We have juft mentioned concerning the *Nervous Liquor,* but alfo with refpect to all the other Parts, as well Fluid as Solid. For *Action* does neceffarily by Degrees impair the Springs and Organs ; and in *Motion* fomething is continually abraded and ftruck off from the Diftractile Fibres, which cannot otherwife be reftored than by their being at reft from *Tenfion.* Befides that, fuch a regular and fteady *Courfe* of the Blood, as we have obferved to be in *Sleep,* is by far more fit and proper for Nutrition, or an Appofition of Parts to the Veffels, which an uneven *Hurry* of It is more apt to tear off and wafh away.

The

The Cafe being thus, it is very plain that whatfoever can induce fuch a Difpofition of the Fluids and Mufcular Parts of the Body, as this We have defcribed, will fo far caufe *Sleepinefs*. And in like manner, when any thing interpofes and hinders this Compofednefs and Tranquillity, the removing of the *Impediment* will be the caufing of *Sleep* ; inafmuch as this is only reducing the Animal *Œconomy* to its right State, in which by natural Order there muft be a Succeffion of Sleeping and Waking.

Thus it appears how neceffarily continued Exercifes do make Us *Sleepy*, fince Thefe do exhauft the Juice of the Nerves ; that is, both leffen its Influx into the Organs of Motion, and incline the Mind not to determine it any longer that way, upon the account of the Pain and Uneafinefs, with which too violent a Tenfion of the Parst is always attended ; which therefore we muft needs defire to Relax, or lay to *Reft*.

That *Sleepinefs* which follows upon a fulnefs of the Stomach after Eatting or Drinking, is owing to a different Caufe ; and does indeed fo nearly fall in with the Effects of *Opiate* Medicines, that it requires a particular Confideration.

As

As *Hunger*, or the Emptiness of the Stomach, is a painful Sensation; so the satisfying or removing of *This*, is a pleasing or agreeable One. Now all *Pain* is a *Stimulus* upon the Part affected; and This, we all know, being attended with Contractions of the pained Membranes, causes a greater Afflux than ordinary of the Nervous Juice that way. On the other Hand, *Pleasure*, or a delightful Sensation in any part, is accompanied with a smooth Undulation, and easie Reflux of the Liquor of the Nerves towards the Brain. This is, as it were, the *Entertainment* of the Mind, with which being *Taken up*, it does not Determine the Spirits to the Organs of Motion; That is, there is such a *Relaxation* of the Muscular Fibres, and such a Disposition of the Nervous Fluid, as we have observed to be necessary to Sleep.

This is the Reason of that *Chilliness* in the Limbs, which we commonly Complain of after a good Feast.

If it seem strange that a Pleasure in the Stomach should so powerfully Influence the Mind; let it be considered, on the other Hand, how violent Effects, an uneasie and disagreeable Sense in the same Part does produce; what a terrible Ago-ny ny Two or Three Grains of *Crocus Metallorum* throws the whole Fabrick into; how readily the Fluid of the Nerves is with a more than Ordinary *Impetus* determin'd and commanded into the Muscles of the Stomach and *Abdomen*, in order to throw off the Enemy, and remove the ungrateful Sensation.

Now the Consequences which we have ascribed to a pleasing Sense in this Part, are only just the contrary of these we find the opposite Affection of Pain induces. And indeed *Pleasure* and *Pain* are Two great Springs of Action in the Animal Œconomy; The Changes they make in the Fabrick are the Causes of many Effects which seem surprising, because we do not regard the Mechanism by which they are produced: but these must be more considerable in the Stomach than any where else; This Part being, for very wise Purposes, of so acute a *Feeling*, that some Philosophers have for this Reason thought It to be the Seat of the Soul.

Besides this Consideration, We must take notice that, the Stomach being distended with Food, presses upon the descending *Trunk* of the *Aorta,* and thus causes a greater Fulness of the Vessels in the

upper

upper Parts; whereupon the Brain is loaded, or the Derivation of Spirits into the Nerves diminished, and *Unactivity* or *Drowsiness* insues. From hence proceed Those *Flushings* in the Face, Redness, &c. after plentiful Eating or Drinking, most Visible in Those whose Vessels are Lax and Weak, as in Exhausted and Hectick Persons they more especially are.

Thus we may, without the Assistance of the *New Chyle* entring into the Vessels, account for that Inclination to Sleep which follows upon a full Stomach; Tho' we must also allow the Distension from *This* to be a considerable Cause of the same Effect; But this does not happen immediately, nay, sometimes perhaps not within Two or Three Hours after Eating; and therefore the sudden *Drowsiness* must (as well as the present Refreshment and Reviving which Meat gives) be chiefly owing to some more speedy Alteration.

We come then in the next Place to *Opium* it self; The Chymical *Analysis* of which (a) does out of One Pound afford of a Volatile *Spirit* of the like Nature with that drawn from Harts-horn, Five Oun-

(a) Vid. *Pitcarn. de Circulatione Sanguinis in animalibus,* §. 20.

L   ces

ces and Five Drachms; of a fætid *Oil*,
One Ounce Two Drachms and a half;
of *Caput Mortuum*, smelling like Spirit of
Harts-horn, Seven Ounces and Six
Drachms.

The Virtues therefore of *Opium* are
owing to a volatile *Alcaline* Salt, intimately mixt and combin'd with an Oily,
Sulphureous Substance. The Effects of
which We must consider, first of all upon the Stomach, and afterwards, when
they have passed the *Primæ Viæ*, upon the
Arterial Fluid it self

An agreeable Sensation produced in the
Stomach, together with a Distension of
Its Membranes, we observed before to be
the Cause of that Sleepiness to which we
are so prone after Eating. The *One* of
These ingages the Mind, the *Other* acts
upon the Body. For Pleasure amuses
the Soul, as it were, so that It does not
Think, or exercise it self about any outward Objects; that is, Is inclined to Rest.
And the Fulness of the Vessels in the Brain
Checks and Hinders, in some Measure,
the Derivation of the Nervous Juice into
the Organs, *&c.*

Now They who take a moderate Dose
of *Opium*, especially if not long accustom-
ed

ed to It, are fo Tranfported with the
pleafing Senfe It induces, that They are,
as They oftentimes exprefs themfelves,
in Heaven; and tho' They do not always Sleep, (which proceeds from the
Prefentation of pleafing Images to the
Mind being fo ftrong, that like Dreams
they do over-ingage the Fancy, and fo interrupt the State of Reft) yet they do however injoy fo perfect an Indolence and
Quiet, that no Happinefs in the World
can furpafs the Charms of this agreable
Extafie.

Thus We have from this Medicine, but
in a far more eminent Degree, all thofe
Effects which we obferved to follow upon that grateful Senfe in the Stomach,
which a moderate Fulnefs produces.
For no Bodies are fo fit and able pleafing-
ly to affect our fenfile Membranes, as
Thofe which confift of Volatile Parts,
whofe activity is tempered and allayed by
the fmoothnefs of fome Lubricating and
Oily ones; which by lightly Rarefying
the Juices of the Stomach, and caufing a
pleafant Titillation of Its Nervous Coat,
will induce an agreable *Plenitude*, and
entertain the Mind with Ideas of Satif-
faction and Delight.

The

The Cafe being thus, We eafily fee upon what Mechanifm the other Virtues of *Opium* do depend, Its Eafing Pains, Checking Evacuations, *&c.* not only in that the Mind being taken up with a pleafing Senfe, is diverted from a difagreable *One* ; But all Pain being attended with a Contraction of the Part, That Relaxation of the Fibres which is now caufed, eludes and deftroys the Force of the *Stimulus*.

In like manner in immoderate Secretions there is moft commonly an Irritation of the Organs, the Removal of which will abate the Difcharge. And herein lies the *Incraffating* Quality of this Medicine, in that the Twitching Senfe upon the Membranes of the Lungs, Bowels, *&c.* being now leffened, the fharp Humor is fuffered to lodge there in a greater quantity, before it is fo troublefome as to be thrown off and expell'd ; it being all one as if there were no Irritation of the Part, if the uneafie Senfe thereof be not regarded by the Mind.

Thefe Effects will all be heightened by the Mixture of the *Opiate* Particles with the *Blood* ; Which is hereupon Rarefied, and Diftends its Veffels, efpecially thofe of the Brain ; and thus does ftill to a

greater

greater Degree leffen the Influx of the Nervous Fluid to the Parts, by prefling upon the little *Tubuli*, or Canals, thro' which it is derived.

This is the Reafon of that *Difficulty of Breathing*, which they do for a time Experience who take thefe kind of Medicines ; This Symptom being infeparable from the Rarefaction of the Blood in the Lungs.

From hence it appears, that the Action of *Opium* is very Analogous to that of other Volatile Spirits, only that a fmall Portion of It has a force equal to that of a greater quantity of moft of Them.

This is very evident in Thofe who accuftom Themfelves to take large Dofes of It ; as the *Turks* and *Perfians* do to that Degree, that it is no uncommon thing there to Eat a Drachm or Two at a time ; for the Effects of It in Them are no other than downright *Drunkennefs* ; upon which account (*b*) it is as common a Saying with Them, and on the fame Occafion, *He has eat Opium* ; as with Us, *He has drank too much Wine*.

Neither indeed do They otherwife bear fuch large quantities of It, than our *Tip-*

(b) Vid. *Belon. Voyag.* lib. 3. c. 15.

plers

plers will a great deal of *Brandy* ; that is, by habituating themfelves to It by degrees, beginning with fmall Dofes, and requiring ftill more and more to raife themfelves to the fame *Pitch.* Juft as *Galen (c)* tells Us of a Woman at *Athens*, who by a gradual Ufe had brought her felf to Take, without any hurt, a confiderable quantity of *Cicuta* or Hemlock. Which Inftance is the more to our Purpofe, becaufe *Nic. Fontanus (d)* knew one who being Recovered of the Plague, and wanting Sleep, did, with very good Effect, eat *Hemlock* for fome time, till falling Ill again of a Fever, and having left off the Ufe of this Remedy, He indeavoured to procure Reft by repeated Dofes of *Opium*, which (Nature having been accuftomed to a ftronger Alterative) had no Operation, till the help of *Cicuta* was again call'd in with defired Succefs.

It is a fufficient Confirmation of all this Reafoning, that *Profper Alpinus (e)* obferved among the *Egyptians*, thofe who had been accuftom'd to *Opium*, and were faint and languid thro' want of It, (as Drinkers are if they have not their

---

(c) *Simpl. Medicam. Facult.* l. 3. c. 18.
(d) *Refponf. & Curat. Medic.* p. 162.
(e) *Medicin. Ægypt.* l. 4. c. 1.

Spirits)

Spirits) to be recovered, and put into the same State of Indolence and Pleasure, by large Doses of *Cretic Wine* made hotter by the Infusion of *Pepper*, and the like strong *Aromatics*.

Nor is it perhaps amiss to remark, that in *Maniacal* People, as is frequently obferv'd, a Quadruple Dose of *Opium* will scarce produce any considerable Effect: Now in Persons so affected, the Mind is deeply ingaged and taken up with some *Images* or other, as Love, Anger, &c. so that it is not to be so easily moved or diverted by those pleasing Representations which it would attend to at another time, and upon which the Virtues of this Medicine do in a great measure depend. Besides this, those who are *Maniacal* do to a Wonder bear the Injuries of Cold, Hunger, &c. and have a prodigious degree of Muscular Force, which argues the Texture of their *Blood* to be very strong, and the Cohæsion of its *Globules* great ; so that the Spirituous Parts of the *Opiate* cannot make that Disjunction and Rarefaction of this Fluid in Them, which it does in ordinary Bodies and Constitutions.

Many are the Immprovements which might be made of this Theory, with re-

lation

lation to the Practice of Phyfick ; but thefe will be obvious enough to one inftructed in the Animal *Œconomy.*

To conclude then as to the Subject in Hand, it is very plain that there needs no more to make *Opium* prove Deftructive or a *Poifon,* than to take too great a quantity of It ; for then It muft Inflame the Sto-mach, and Rarefie the Blood to fuch a Degree, that the Veffels cannot again re-cover their Tone, whereupon Apoplectic Symptoms, *&c.* will infue.

To be convinced of this, I forced into the Stomach of a fmall Dog about half a Drachm of Crude *Opium* diffolved in Boiling Water. He quickly Vomited It up with a great quantity of Frothy Spit-tle ; but repeating the Trial, by holding up his Head, and beating him, I made him retain Three or Four Dofes, inter-mitting between each about a quarter of an Hour ; when he had thus taken, as I could guefs, near Two Drachms, I watch'd him about an Hour, then he began to Sleep, but prefently ftarted up with Con-vulfions, fell into univerfal Tremblings, his Head conftantly twitch'd and fhaking, he breath'd fhort and with labour, loft intirely the Ufe firft of his hinder Legs, and then of the fore ones, which were

ftiff

ftiff and rigid like Sticks. As he lay Snorting, to haften his End, I was giving him more of the Solution, but on a fudden his Limbs grew limber, and He Died.

Opening his *Stomach*, I found It wonderfully diftended, tho' empty of every thing but fome Water and *Opium*; parcels of Frothy *Mucus* fwimming in It; the infide was as clean as if fcraped and wafhed from all the Slime of the Glands, with fome Rednefs here and there, as in a beginning Inflammation. The *Pylorus* was Contracted. The Blood-Veffels of the Brain were very full; and I took out a large Grume of Concrete Blood from the upper part of It, cutting into the *Sinus Longitudinalis*, as is not uncommon in Apopleftic Carcaffes; but found no extravafated *Serum* in the *Ventricles*, nor among any of the Membranes.

As to the Cure of fuch a Cafe; befides other Evacuations, Acid Medicines and Lixivial Salts muft certainly do Service; thefe by their *Diuretic* force caufing a Depletion of the Veffels. This is the Foundation upon which *Starky* compounded his *Pacific Pill.* Generous *Wine*, which the Ancients gave for an Antidote, can be no other ways ufeful, than as It
diffolves

diffolves the *Refinous* Clammy Part of the *Opium* fticking to the Coats of the Stomach, and fo forwards its Expulfion by other Helps, which caufe a Contraction of the Mufcular Fibres.

ESSAY

ESSAY V.

OF

Venomous Exhalations

FROM THE

EARTH,

Poisonous Airs and Waters.

BESIDES thefe already treated of, there is yet another way of being *Poifoned*, and that is by *Venomous Steams* and *Exhalations*, or a *Poifonous Air* taken into the Body by the Breath.

This

This is notorious enough, and Authors do upon many Occasions make mention of it; but when they come to explain the particular manner how this Kills, they moſt commonly reduce it to ſome of the *Poiſons* which prove deſtructive by being admitted into the Stomach, alledging that Malignant Fumes and Airs are therefore fatal, becauſe impregnated with *Arſenical Mercurial*, and the like, Deleterious Μιάσμᾶτα or Particles, they do convey theſe into the Blood; which being of a very Corroſive Nature, muſt neceſſarily do hurt both to the Fluid and Solid Parts.

And indeed that the *Fumes* of theſe ſame Minerals are very pernicious, and Air fill'd with their Atoms very unfit for Reſpiration, is moſt certain; but to argue from hence, that all deadly *Vapours* and Malignant *Airs* owe their Miſchief to theſe only, is too fond and illgrounded a Conceit; ſince upon a due Enquiry it will appear, that there may be, and are, *Mortiferous Exhalations* from the Earth, infecting the Air, of a Nature ſo different from any of thoſe *Poiſons,* that the very Subſtance from which they ariſe may not be at all hurtful, tho' taken into the Stomach it ſelf.

Venomous

Venomous Steams and Damps from the Earth the *Latins* in one Word call'd *Mephites* (*a*).

This, as many other *Tuscan* Words, comes from a *Syriac* Theme, which signifies to blow or breathe (*b*).

And in ancient times several Places were notorious for 'em ; so the *Mephitis* of *Hierapolis* was very Famous, of which *Cicero*, *Galen*, but more particularly, and from his own Sight and Knowledge *Strabo* (*c*) makes mention.

Such another was the *Specus Corycius* in *Cilicia*, which upon the account of its stinking deadly Air, such as is thought to proceed from the Mouth of *Dragons*, which the Poets give to *Typhon*, was call'd *Cubile Typhonis*. This *Pompon. Mela* (*d*) describes ; and it is indeed as ancient as *Homer* (*e*) ; for *Arima*, in which he places it, was, as *Eustathius* says, a Mountain of *Cilicia*.

(a) *Virgil* Æn. 7. v. 8.
———— *Sævamq; exhalat. opaca Mephitim.*
Vid. Servium, ibid.
(b) *Scaliger. Conject. in Varron.*
(c) **Lib.** 13.
(d) *De Situ Orb.* l. 1. c. 13.
(e) 'Εἰν 'Αρίμοις ὅθι φασὶ Τυφῶεὸς ἔμμεναι εὐνάς.
Il. B. v. 783.

Neither are fuch *Fumes* as thefe infre-
quent Now-a-days; and though moftly
taken notice of in Mines, Pits, and o-
ther Subterraneous Places, yet they are
fometimes met with in the Surface of the
Earth too, efpecially in Countries fruit-
ful of Minerals, or pregnant with Imbow-
elled Fires; fuch are *Hungary* and *Italy*,
which latter (as *Seneca* (*f*) obferves) has
always been more than any other remarkable for 'em.

I fhall therefore, having had the opportunity of making fome Remarks upon
One the moft Famous of all in thofe
Parts, give as good an account as I can of
That, and its manner of Killing; which
tho' I dare not affirm to be univerfally
applicable to any *Mephitis* whatfoever,
yet feems plainly to be the Cafe of moft
of 'em; and where it is not, this fimple
Mifchief will only be found to be complicated with another; and then fome extraordinary Symptoms or Appearances in
the Animals kill'd, will eafily make a
Difcovery of the Additional Venom and
Malignity.

This Celebrated *Mofeta* taken notice
of, (or at leaft fome other hereabouts)

(f) *Nat. Quaft.* l. 6. c. 28.

even

even in the time of *Pliny* (*g*), is about Two Miles diftant from *Naples*, juft by the *Lago d' Agnano*, in the way to *Pozzoli* or *Puteoli*, and is commonly call'd *la Grotta de Cani*, becaufe the Experiment of its deadly Nature is frequently made upon *Dogs*; tho' it be as certainly fatal to any other Animal, if it come within the reach of its Vapour; for *Charles the Eighth of* France prov'd it fo upon an *Afs*; and two *Slaves* put into it by order of *D. Pietro di Toledo*, Viceroy of *Naples*, with their Heads held down to the Earth, were both kill'd (*h*).

'Tis a fmall *Grotta* at the Foot of a little Hill, about Eight Foot high, Twelve long, and Six broad; from the Ground arifes a thin, fubtle, warm *Fume*, vifible enough to a difcerning Eye, which does not fpring up in little parcels here and there, but is one continued Steam, covering the whole Surface of the bottom of the Cave; and has this remarkable difference from common Vapours, that it does not, like Smoak, difperfe it felf into the Air, but quickly after its rife falls back again, and returns to the Earth; the

(*g*) Nat. Hift. *l.* 2. c. 93.
(*h*) *L. di Capoa delle Mofet.* pag. 37.

Colour

Colour of the fides of the *Grotta* being the meafure of its Afcent; for fo far it is of a darkifh Green, but higher, only common Earth, and this is about Ten Inches. And therefore as my felf found no Inconvenience by ftanding in it, fo no Animal if its Head be kept above this Mark is in the leaft injured : But when (as the manner is) a Dog, or any other Creature, is forcibly held below it, or by reafon of its fmalnefs can't hold its Head above it, It prefently, like one ftunn'd, lofes all Motion, falls down as Dead, or in a Swoon, the Limbs convuls'd and trembling, till at laft no more fign of Life appears than a very weak and almoft Infenfible beating of the Heart and Arteries, which if the Animal be left there a little longer, quickly ceafes too, and then the Cafe is Irrecoverable; But if fnatch'd out, and laid in the open Air, foon comes to Life again, and fooner if thrown into the adjacent *Lake.*

In this fhort, but accurate, Hiftory of the *Grotta de Cani,* I have fet dow thofe Particulars which do not only diftinguifh *Mephitical* Exhalations from common and innocent Fumes, but alfo give hints fufficient, I think, Mechanically to determine the Reafon and Manner of their furprifing Effects.   And

And not to spend time in refuting the Opinions of Others, I shall only take Notice, that here can be no suspicion of any true *Venom* or real Poison; if there was, it were impossible that Animals taken out of the *Grotta*, should so immediately recover the Effects of it, without any remaining appearance of Faintness and Sickness, or such like Symptoms as those suffer who have been breathing in an Air impregnated with malignant corrosive *Effluvia*. Besides, that the Venomous Corpuscles would certainly, in some Degree at least, infect the Air in the upper Part of the Cave, which continues pure, and fit for Respiration. Neither indeed after what manner soever this Poison be imagin'd to Act, whether by dissolving or coagulating the Blood, could its Efficacy be so sudden and momentaneous, without some Marks of it in the Creatures kill'd, when opened, which yet do discover nothing of this Nature extraordinary, neither in the Fluid, nor in the Solid Parts.

In order therefore to understand wherein this deadly quality Consists; I say in the first Place, that Life, so far as it respects the Body, is, in one Word, the *Circulation* of the Blood; that is, its Mo-

M   tion

tion in *Conical* Diſtractile Veſſels from the
Heart to the Extreme Parts, and its Re-
turn to the Heart again by the ſame Ca-
nals inverted ; For 'tis upon this that all
Animal Functions, all Senſe and Motion
Voluntary and Involuntary, do depend ;
ſo that the Regularity of this Courſe is the
Meaſure of Health, or the moſt perfect
Life, as its various Irregularities are the
Occaſions of Sickneſs and Diſeaſes, or a
beginning Death.

Now all the Animal Operations and
Offices which proceed from this Circulati-
on, are the Effects of ſeveral Secretions
of Liquors of very different Natures out
of the ſame Fluid Maſs ; It was therefore
abſolutely neceſſary that the Blood, before
It be diſtributed to the Organs, ſhould be
ſo comminuted and broken, as that no
Cohæſion of its Parts ſhould hinder the
Separation of theſe *Juices* from It, when it
Arrives with a determinate Force at the
Orifices of the Secretory Veſſels.

This Work is done in Its Paſſage thro'
the *Lungs*, by the repeated Compreſſion
of the Air in thoſe *Bladders* upon the Arteries, with wonderful Contrivance di-
ſpers'd among 'em (*a*). Herein lies the

(*a*) Vid. *Malpigh. de Pulmon.*

Uſe

Ufe and Neceffity of *Refpiration* ; and the fudden Mifchief of Stopping it, in that the whole Mafs of Blood being to pafs this way, upon a Check here, there prefently infues a Stagnation, that is, a Ceffation of all Animal Functions, or Death ; Which will be the more fpeedy, if not only no Air is infpired, but a Fluid of a quite different Nature from It fucceeds in its Place.

Wherefore it muft be obferved, that this good Effect of the Air is performed by its *Elafticity* ; And that no Fluid whatfoever, that we know befides, is *Elaftic*, at leaft to any confiderable Degree, that is, has a faculty of expanding and and dilating it felf when compreffed ; No, not *Water*, as near as That is thought to approach to Air in its Nature.

And now as to the prefent Cafe, I took notice before that this *Vapour* is one continued and uninterrupted *Steam*, and that quickly after Its rife it falls down again ; that is, that it has little or no mixture of Air with It, or no Elafticity ; and is, on the other Hand, very heavy, when forfaken by the Force of *Heat* that drove it upwards.

So that I make no Queftion, but that Animals in this Place do inftead of Air

M 2   infpire

inspire *Mineral Fumes*, that is, a thin watery Vapour, impregnated with such Particles as do, when united together, compose solid and heavy Masses; which is so far from helping the Course of the Blood thro' the *Lungs*, that it rather expels the Air out of the *Vesiculæ*, and straitens the Passage of the Blood Vessels, by its too great Gravity; whereupon the *Bladders* are relaxed and subside, and the Circulation is immediately Interrupted. But if the Animal be in time removed out of this *Steam*, that small Portion of Air which does after every Exspiration remain in the *Vesiculæ*, may be powerful enough to drive out this Noxious Fluid; especially if the Head of the Creature be held downwards, that so its Gravity may forward its Expulsion; or It be thrown into Water, which by assisting, upon the account of its Coldness, the Contraction of the Fibres, promotes the retarded Circle of the Blood; as we every Day experience in a *Deliquium Animi*, or Swooning Fit.

Tho' if this Stagnation be continued too long, no Art can renew Life, no more than in One perfectly strangled; nor will the *Lake of Agnano* it self be of any Service; which shews that there is no

singular

fingular Virtue in That Water beyond any other ; nor is it, as fome have fondly Imagin'd, a Peculiar Antidote to the Poi-fon of the *Grotta.*

The bad Effects of fuch *Fumes* as This will be the more certain, becaufe the in-fpired Mineral Particles twitch and irritate the Membranes, which are hereupon con-tracted to that Degree, as not to be able to recover their Tone, and fo the Force and Action of the *Lungs* is quite loft.

It appears from all This not to be at all neceffary to make any farther Enquiry into the particular Nature of thefe Mine-ral Particles, fince they do in this Cafe act chiefly by their *Gravity*, which is com-mon to 'em all. Tho' indeed the *Greenifh* Colour of the Earth, together with its *Subacid* Tafte, very much (as *L. di Ca-poa* obferves) like to that of the *Phlegm* of *Vitriol*, feem to declare them, if not altogether, yet principally at leaft, to be *Vitriolick.*

To conclude this Part of our Difcourfe ; I think it a fufficient Confirmation of this Reafoning, that in *Frogs* kill'd in this *Grotta*, the *Bladders* of the Lungs (more vifible otherwife and diftinct in thefe Creatures than in moft others) were found fubfided, and quite empty

of

of Air (*c*). But if any one defires a farther Proof, he may, according to thefe Principles, make (as *Lionardo di Capoa* (*d*) did) an Artificial *Mephitis*; for if *Antimony*, *Bifmuth*, or any other fuch Mineral be finely powdered, and moiftened with *Aqua Fortis*, or *Spirit* of *Nitre*, there will arife a great Heat, and a thick dark Smoak, in which, as in the *Grotta de Cani*, Torches are extinguifh'd, and Animals, tho' but flowly, ftifled and kill'd. And this Effect will be more fenfible, and equal to the moft Violent *Mephites*, if the *Antimony* or *Marcafite* be mix'd with *Bitumen*, and the *Spirit* of *Nitre*, or *Aqua Fortis*, intirely depurated from all its *Phlegm*.

And thus I have fhewn how Death may enter at the Noftrils, tho' nothing properly *Venomous* be infpired. It were perhaps no difficult Matter to make it appear, how a leffer Degree of this Mifchief may produce Effects, tho' feemingly very different from thefe now mention'd, yet in reality of the fame Pernicious Na-

(*c*) *Vid. L. di Capoa Mofet.* pag. 40.
(*d*) Pag. 128.

ture ; I mean, how such an alteration of
the common Air as renders it in a manner *Mephitical*, that is, increases its
Gravity, and lessens its *Elasticity*, (which
is done by too much Heat, and at the
same time too great a Proportion of watery and other grosser Particles mixt with
it) may be the Cause of *Epidemic* Diseases, and, it may be, more especially of
those, which by Reason of their untoward Symptoms, are usually call'd *Malignant*.

For it is very Remarkable, that *Hippocrates (a)* observ'd the Constitution of
the Air, which preceded *Pestilential* Fevers, to be great *Heats*, attended with much
Rain and Southern Winds ; and *Galen (b)*
takes Notice, that no other than a *moist*
and *hot* Temperament of the Air
brings the *Plague* it self ; and that
the Duration of this Constitution is
the Measure of the Violence of the
Pestilence. *Lucretius (c)* is of the same
Mind, for in his admirable Description of the *Plague* of *Athens*, These

---

(a) *Epidem.* l. 2, & 3.
(b) *De Temperament.* l. 1. c. 4. & *Commentar. in* E, i-
dem. l. 3.
(c) L. 6. v. 1098.

Diseases,

Difeafes, fays He, *either come from the Air, or arife from the Earth,*

———*Ubi* Putrorem humida *nacta eft Intempeftivis* Pluviifq; & Solibus *icta.*

In fhort, the general *Hiftories* of *Epidemic* Diftempers, do almoft conftantly Confirm thus much, and would have done it more, if the vain Notion of *Occult Venoms* had not prepoffefs'd the Minds of Authors, and made Them regardlefs of the manifeft Caufes.

And this is notorious enough in thofe Countries where *Malignant* Difeafes are moft rife ; Thus it is a very common Obfervation in the *Eaft-Indies,* that during the dry Heats the Seafon is Healthful, but when the Rains fall immediately upon the Hot Weather, then *untoward Fevers* begin to threaten.

The fame is obferv'd in *Africa* ; for (as *Joan, Leo (d)* relates) if *Showers* fall there during the Sultry *Heats* of *July* and *Auguft,* the *Plague* and Peftilential Fevers infue thereupon, with which whofoever is infected hardly efcapes.

(d) Hiftor. Afric. *l.* 1. *c.* 1. Vid. Purchas's *Pilgrims, i.* 6. *c.* 1.

And

And here I might, by Reflecting on the Use and Neceſſity of *Reſpiration*, and the particular manner of performing It, (of which I have hinted ſomething already) and conſidering withal the true Nature of *Fevers*, eaſily ſhew how ſuch a Conſtitution of the Air, as this is, muſt neceſſarily produce ſuch Effects; might run over the *Propoſitions* of *Bellini*; which *as* they do plainly evince *Malignant* and *Peſtilential Fevers* to be owing to a viſcid and tenacious *Lentor* or Slime, which at firſt obſtructs the Capillary Arteries, and afterwards being diſſolved by Heat, Ferments with the Blood, and changes it into a Maſs unequally Fluid and Glutinous, and therefore unfit for all the Operations of the Animal Œconomy; *ſo* it would be no uneaſie Task to prove, that Air at the ſame time *Hot* and *Moiſt*, being leſs able to comminute and break the Arterial Fluid in the *Lungs* than is neceſſary, in order to prepare it for Secretions, it is no wonder, if when the Blood paſſing thro' the Capillary Veſſels arrives at the Secretory Organs, the Cohæſion of its Parts not being ſufficiently removed, inſtead of deriving ſeveral Juices out of it into the Glands, it leaves its moſt Glutinous and Viſcid Parts ſticking about the Orifices of theſe thefe Veffels; which tho' they may at firft be wafh'd away by the repeated Impulfes of the fucceeding Blood, yet the Caufe continuing, and thefe Strokes growing ftill Weaker and Weaker, (from a leffer quantity of Spirits being feparated, and hence a more languid Contraction of the Heart) Thefe Obftructions are increas'd to that Degree as not to be remov'd, till by the Violent Agitation of a greater Heat, this *Slimy Mucus* is thrown into the Blood again, and there in the Nature of a *Ferment* fo difturbs its *Mixture*, and changes its *Compages*, as to make it a Fluid of quite different Properties, that is, altogether unfit for the fame Functions or Offices.

This Effect will be the more certain, becaufe a damp Air upon the furface of the Body checks infenfible Perfpiration, fo that a great quantity of this being detained, the Obftructions are ftill greater in the fmall Tubes; whereas indeed upon the Account of a more than ordinary Heat, this Difcharge ought now to be in an increafed Proportion.

Such a Difpofition of the Blood as this the Ancients call'd *Putrid*; and to fpeak plainly, it is a Beginning Stagnation, with a Succeeding Heat and Fermentation.

Nor

Nor would it be amiss here to take notice, how unjustly some Authors, having quitted the Consideration of *plain Causes*, for *Occult Venoms* and *Deleterium quid*, have brought in the θεῖον τι (*something Divine*) of *Hippocrates* (e) to favour their fond *Hypothesis*; tho' His best Interpreter *Galen*, understood by this Expression no such thing as they mean; but on the other Hand, only the *manifest Constitution of the ambient Air*, such as himself has described in his *Aphorisms* (f), and which is exactly the same with That We have been discoursing of.

And therefore not only does *Minadous* (g) rightly Remark, that in his whole *Epidemics*, *Hippocrates* never once mentions any *Venom* or Poison as the Cause of *Malignant* Diseases; But the Divine Old Man himself in another *Treatise* (b) expresly teaches Us, that *All Maladies do equally, or one as much as another, proceed from the Gods, there being nothing more Divine in this than in that, each acknowledging its own Natural and Manifest Cause.*

(e) *Prognostic.* 1. & *Galen. Comment.*
(f) Sect. 3. Aph. 11.
(g) *De Febre Malign* l. 1. c. 11.
(h) *De Aere, Locis, & Aquis.*

But

But I willingly wave infifting upon thefe Heads, as well as the Hints which might be taken from this Theory, of fome Ufe perhaps in the Cure of thefe Diftempers; and leave it to our Phyficians to judge upon how good Grounds They do, in Cafes of this Nature, under the Notion of *Alexipharmics*, give fuch Medicines as raife a great Heat both in the Stomach and Blood; only praying Them to take Care, leaft while They are ingaging the Animal Spirits in War with *Malignities*, They do fend Treacherous *Auxiliaries* to the fuppofed weak *Party*; that is, that they either raife new Tumults and Diforders of worfe Confequence than the Original Mifchief; or at leaft, by clogging the Wheels, and throwing Duft upon the Springs of the fineft Machine in the Creation, do check and interrupt the Action of Nature (*i*), when 'tis imploy'd about the moft Nice and *Critical* Work.

Neither can I, tho' an occafion be fairly offer'd, by any means be induced to intermeddle in the Controverfie of thofe Gentlemen, who by the help of Two Words are made Mafters both of Philofophy and Phyfick; I mean, the Vio-

(i) Φύσιες Νέσων ἰητροί. *Hippocr.* Epid. 6.

lent

lent Affertors of *Acid* and *Alkali*. Thefe
fcanty Principles fall infinitely fhort of
that vaft Variety there is in the Works of
Nature; However, for Their Sakes who
are as yet Advanc'd no farther, I will advife the Contending Parties, (becaufe little good is got by Quarrelling) to Think
of an Union, and if They can find no
Remedies but out of thefe Two Tribes,
to make Ufe of fuch as refult from a prudent Mixture of fome out of Each. If
this *Project* does not take, to Refolve
however on both fides, To Diftinguifh
the differing Times of the fame Difeafe,
and know, that *as*, on the one Hand, *Acid*
Medicines are oftentimes as certainly hurtful in the latter End, as they do fervice
in the Beginning of the Fever; *fo*, on
the other, thofe which are *Alcalious* muft
neceffarily for the fame Reafon do mifchief in the firft Periods, for which they
are profitable in the laft Days of the Diftemper.

By what Mechanifm this comes to pafs,
They will eafily underftand, when they
have learn'd what Alteration fuch things
as thefe are do make in the humane Body; nor will it then be a difficult Matter
to convince Them, That He is equally a
fond Slave to an *Hypothefis*, who becaufe

Acids

Acids are sometimes of great Service in Fevers, concludes that their Origine is *Alcalious*; as He who knowing that Stagnating and Fermenting Juices do easily turn to *Acidity*, from thence Argues that *Alcalies* are the only Cure of this Stagnation and Ferment.

But Dr. *Pitcarne* (*k*) has abundantly demonstrated the Weakness of These Men's Reasonings, and the Vanity of such Immechanical Theories.

And here I would put a Period to this Part of the Discourse, were it not that these Distempers being sometimes *Contagious*, and *Contagion* being justly reputed a real *Poison*, it may be worth the while to examine a little what This is, and wherein it consists; more especially, because some may perhaps be apt to think This to be an Argument of an *Occult Venom*'s being the First and Original Cause.

We are therefore to take Notice, that when a *Fever* is communicated by way of *Infection* from one already Diseased, this most commonly happens in the latter End of the Distemper, that is, (as we before discoursed concerning the *Hydrophobia*)

(k) *Differtatio de opera quam præftant corpora acida vel alcalica in Curatione Morborum.*

when

when the Fermenting Blood is throwing off great quantities of its Active Fermentative Particles upon the Glands of the moſt conſtant and eaſie Secretion; ſuch are thoſe in the Surface of the Body, and the Mouth and Stomach; By this means therefore the Liquid of inſenſible Perſpiration, and the Sweat is impregnated with theſe μάσμᾳῖα, and thus the ambient Air becomes fill'd with 'em; ſo that not only, (as *Bellini* Argues (*l*),) may ſome of theſe *Effluvia* inſinuate themſelves into the Blood of a ſound Perſon thro' the Pores of the outward Skin, but alſo in Inſpiration thro' the Membrane of the Lungs; for He has in another Place (*m*) demonſtrated how the Air, or ſomething from It, may this way come to be mix'd with the Arterial Fluid; And thus the like *Ferment* will be rais'd Here, as was in the Originally Diſtemper'd Subject.

This may be *One*, but there is perhaps *another* yet more dangerous manner of *Infection*, and that is, by the Breath of the Diſeaſed taken in by a By-ſtander, eſpecially in the laſt Moments, ſeizing the *Stomach*, and fixing a *Malignity* There.

(*l*) *De Febrib.* Prop. 27.
(*m*) *De Motu Cordis*, Prop. 9.

For it is upon this Score, that Those who are *Infected* do prefently complain of an extreme Pain and *Naufea* in the upper Orifice of the Stomach; and that all Authors do agree in the admirable Ufe of *Vomits* timely given in this Cafe; Thefe by their Stimulating Force removing the very *Minera* of the Difeafe; and likewife that, oftentimes in *Peftilential* Illneffes, the *Stomach* when open'd has been found Gangren'd and Mortify'd. This made *Van Helmont* (*n*), who had obferv'd this Part in one kill'd by a *Plague Infection*, perforated and eroded in feveral Places, no otherwife than He had feen in one Poifon'd by *Arfenick*, conclude, that the Plague for the moft Part begins in the Stomach from a coagulated *Tartar* there.

Herein lies the difference of *Contagion*, from the firft Invafion of Malignant Diftempers; The Effects of the *One* are the Caufe and Beginning of the *Other*; and therefore it is no wonder, if tho' the Symptoms in the former are by a gradual Increafe wrought up to their height, they do however in the latter, even at the very firft, difcover their ill Nature and Vio-

(*n*) *Tumulus Peftis*, pag. m. 163, & 172.

lence,

lence, and, like a reinforc'd Enemy, by furer Strokes make quicker Difpatch. And this alfo is the Reafon of the great Increafe of *Funerals* in Plague Time, in that One Death is thus added to Another.

If it be difficult to explain the particular manner how the *Stomach* comes to be thus affected, We muft not therefore deny Matter of Fact; and may however probably Conjecture, that the laft *Breath* of one Dying of a Malignant Diftemper, proves thus pernicious, in that Thofe fermenting active Particles, which, as we juft now obferv'd, the Blood difcharges upon the Glands of the *Mouth*, *Stomach*, *Lungs*, &c. impregnating the Air in its Paffage thro' thefe; when the fame happens to be immediately infpired by a found Perfon, it may eafily taint the *Salival* Juices in the Mouth, which are very Glutinous, and of a fermenting Nature, and therefore fufceptible enough of *Contagious Effluvia*, but efpecially of fuch as proceed from the fame Liquor infected in the Sick Party. Now the *Spittle* is continually fwallow'd down into the Stomach, and fo will quickly imprefs its *Labes*, or ill Quality, on fo tender and fenfible a Part; that is, will lodge thefe

N   Cor-

Corrofive *Salts*, (for fuch We may fuppofe the Particles of Infection) in the Secretory Ducts; whereupon the Glands being obftructed, little *Tumors* are by the Afflux of their Fluid rais'd here and there, which breaking become fmall *Ulcers*, and produce that difmal Train of Symptoms which we have already related.

And here it may not be amifs to take notice, that all Authors do agree, One great Caufe of *Peftilential* Diftempers, efpecially in Armies and Camps, to be dead Bodies lying expos'd and rotting in the open Air; The Reafon of which is plain from what we have been advancing; For Battels being generally fought in the Summer Time, it is no wonder, if the Heat acting upon the unbury'd *Carcaffes*, and *Fermenting* the Juices, draws forth thofe active Particles, which in great quantities filling the Atmofphere, when they are infpired and let into the Stomach, do affect It after the manner already defcribed.

To illuftrate this Matter, I fhall relate a remarkable Story told Me by the learned Dr. *Baynard*. The Body of a Malefactor was Hung up in Chains in the Country; after a few Months, in very hot Weather it was Sport and Paftime to fome Boys, Playing thereabouts to Swing the Carcafs,

cafs up and down ; One more bold than the Reft ftruck It with his Fift upon the naked Belly, which being outwardly parch'd and dry, and from the falling down of the Humours Swell'd and Tenfe, was eafily burft by the Blow ; out gufh'd a Water fo Corrofive and Fiery, that running down the poor Lad's Arm, it caus'd a Violent *Excoriation,* and a very hard Matter it was to preferve It from being truly mortified. What this *Serum* could do upon the outward Skin, the more Volatile Parts of It would, without all doubt, Effect upon the more tender and fenfible Membranes of the *Stomach,* if a confiderable number of them were fixt there. The Fluids of Humane Bodies being Ranker and more abounding in active Salts than thofe of other Creatures, which are not continually repaired and nourifh'd by the Juices of Animals.

The Way by which *Bad Food,* *ill ripened Fruits* of the Earth, *&c.* do oftentimes produce *Malignant* and *Peftilential* Difeafes, is not very different from *That* by which We have obferv'd Unwholefome Airs to be the Caufe of the like Effects. For the Juices with which Thofe do fupply the Blood being Corrupted, muft necefarily make a Fluid of quite

N 2   other

other Properties than what the Animal Œconomy requires, that is, neither Fit for Nutrition, nor for the Secretion of those Liquors which in the several Organs are to be derived from It ; whereupon the small *Tubes* are obstructed by an unequally Glutinous *Slime*; and it is therefore no wonder, if besides the other Symptoms insuing, *Sore Pustules, Inflammations, Ulcers,* &c. (more common in Fevers from this Cause than in any other,) are raised in the Surface of the Body.

This is the Ground of the common Observation, that a *Famine* is very often succeeded by a *Pestilence.* And This *Calamity* generally begins among the Poorer sort of People, whose Diet to be sure is the worst.

The City of *Surat* in the *East-Indies* is seldom or never free from the Plague ; and yet it is observ'd, that the *English* who Trade there are in no danger of being Infected thereby. Now the Chief of the Natives in this Place are *Banians*, who neither Eat Flesh, nor Drink Wine, but Live very Poorly upon *Herbs, Rice, Water,* &c. and most of the Inhabitants do the like, except Foreigners ; This Poor Fare, together with the Heat of the Climate, makes them so liable to Malignant Distem-

Diftempers; from the Attacks of which
Thofe who Feed well are more Safe and
Secure.

Thus much concerning *Poifonous Exhalations and Airs,* fo far as the Confideration of the *Grotta de' Cani* has led Us on
to enquire into their Effects; for tho'
there may be other Alterations of this
fame Element, differing in their Nature
from this we have infifted upon, and yet
equally Pernicious and Hurtful, yet We
take no Notice of any of them, in regard
that thofe which are from *Arfenical, Mercurial,* and the like *Fumes,* are reducible
to a foregoing *Effay*; and thofe which
are owing to a Change of the known
Properties of the Air, may be eafily explain'd by what has been already delivered in *This.* I fhall therefore rather chufe to make fome Remarks on
the Mifchief of another *Fluid,* which *as*
It is the next in ufe to This we have
been treating of, *fo* the bad Qualities of
it, when it comes to be altered, muft
neceffarily be almoft equally Fatal and
Dangerous.

I mean *Water,* which is of fo conftant
Service, not only for our Drinks, but alfo in preparing of our Flefh and Bread,

that

that it may juftly be faid to be the *Vehicle* of all our Nourifhment ; fo that whenever this happens to put on other Properties than are neceffary to fit it for this Purpofe, it is no wonder if in its Paffage thro' the Body thefe do make fuitable Impreffions there.

Thus at *Paris* (*o*), where the Water of the River *Seine* is fo full of Stony Corpufcles, that even the Pipes through which it is carried, in time are incrufted and ftopt up by 'em, The Inhabitants are more Subject to the *Stone* in the Bladder than in moft other Cities. The fame I obferved in the *Baths* of *Abano*, a few Miles from *Padua*, to that Degree, that it is neceffary very frequently to clear the Wheel of a Mill driven by the Current of thefe Springs, from the great quantity of *petrify'd* Matter with which it is from time to time incumbered.

In like manner, let the grofs Particles with which the *Water* is faturated be of any other Nature, *Metallick*, *Salts*, &c. thefe, according to their various Gravity, the Capacity of Canals, and fuch like Circumftances, will, when they come to circulate in the Animal Body, be by the

(*o*) *Vid. Lifter's* Voyage to *Paris.*

Laws

Laws of Motion depofited in one Part or other. So thofe Mineral Bodies, and Nitrous Salts, which abound in the Snowy Waters of the *Alps,* do fo certainly Stuff and Inlarge the Glands of the Throat in Thofe who Drink 'em, that fcarce any who live there are exempted from this Inconvenience *(a).*

For this Reafon, the Choice of *Water* for Drink among the Ancients was by Weight, the lighteft being preferr'd, as moft free from all Heterogeneous Bodies.

The Cafe therefore of *Poifonous Springs* is, their having Corrofive Corpufcles mixt with their Water, which cannot fail when forfaken in the Canals of the Body of their Vehicle, to do the fame mifchief as they would if taken by themfelves undiluted ; only with this difference, that they may in this form be carried fometimes farther into the Animal Œconomy, and fo having pafs'd the *Primæ Viæ,* difcover their Malignity in fome of the inmoft Receffes. Thus the *Fons Ruber* in *Æthiopia,* mention'd by *Pliny (b),* about which abundance of

(a) *Quis tumidum Guttur miratur in Alpibus.* Juvenal
  Satyr. 13.
(b) Lib. 31. cap. 2.

N 4   native

native *Minium* or *Cinnabar* was found, ſhew'd its ill Effects chiefly on the Brain; and therefore *Ovid (c)*, ſays of it,

——*Si quis Faucibus hauſit*
Aut Furit aut patitur mirum gravitate So-
    porem.

We ſhall not need then to inlarge on this Matter, ſince any of the foremention'd *Mineral Poiſons* may thus impart their deadly quality to Waters; and accordingly there are Inſtances of *Arſenical, Mercurial,* &c. Fountains, of which the Hiſtories may be ſeen in the Collections of the Learned *Baccius (d)*. And one very remarkable in the *Philoſophical Tranſactions (e)*.

But as We before took Notice concerning *Airs,* ſo it may be worth the while to obſerve of *Waters*; that there are ſome Alterations of them, which tho' not properly *Poiſonous,* yet are of ſo great Conſequence in their Effects, that they may very well deſerve to be regarded.

This I ſhall do with reſpect to a great Abuſe, committed in this kind about the

(c) *Metam.* lib. 15.
(d) *De Therm.* lib. 6.
(e) *N°.* 8.

City ; and that is, In the chufing of ftagnating impure *Well-Water* for the *Brewing*
of *Beer*, and making other Drinks. Such
a Fluid indeed has oftentimes a greater
Force and Aptnefs to extract the Tincture
out of *Malt*, than is to be had in the
more innocent and foft Liquor of Rivers ;
but for this very Reafon it ought not,
unlefs upon meer Neceffity, to be made
ufe of ; this quality being owing to the
Mineral Particles and *Aluminous* Salts with
which it is impregnated.

A late *Author* (*f*) by fearching into
the firft Accounts of the Diftemper we
call the *Scurvy*, defcrib'd by *Pliny* (*g*)
and *Strabo* (*h*), under the promifcuous
Names of *Stomacace* and *Scelotyrbe* ; and
examining the Authentick Hiftories of It
in later Years, made by the moft obfer-
ving Phyficians in thofe Countries where
it was unhappily revived, as *Olaus Mag-
nus, Balduinus Ronfeus, J. Wierus, Solomon
Albertus*, &c. finds that the Origine of It
was in all times and places charged upon
the ufe of unwholefome ftagnating *Waters*. Then by comparing together the

---

(*f*) Dr. *J. H. Scelera Aquarum :* Or, a Supplement to
Mr. *Graunt* on the Bills of Mortality.
(*g*) Lib. 25. c. 3.
(*h*) *Geogr.* lib. 6.

Clayie

Clayie Strata of the Earth about the Cities of *London*, *Paris*, and *Amſterdam*, He ſhews that where the Water is worſt, there this Malady is moſt rife. So that He has put it out of all doubt, that moſt of the perplex'd and complicated Symptoms which are ranged under this one general Name, if they do not entirely owe their Birth to the Malignity of this Element, do however acknowledge it to be their main and principal Cauſe.

And indeed *Hippocrates* himſelf, as He has very plainly decipher'd this Diſeaſe (*i*), by the Title of σπλῆνες μέγαλοι, or *great Milts*; ſo he does very particularly in another *Treatiſe* (*k*), take notice, that Drinking of *Stagnating Well-Waters* muſt neceſſarily induce an ill Diſpoſition both of the *Milt* and Belly.

If we enquire into the Reaſon of ſuch ill Effects, we muſt conſider, that *Clay* is a *Mineral Glebe*, and that the groſs Particles and Metallick Salts with which Waters paſſing thro' ſuch a Bottom do abound, are, as Dr. *Liſter* (*l*) obſerves,

(i) *Prorrhet.* l. 2. c. 16.
(k) *De Aere Aquis & Locis, ſub finem.*
(l) *De Fontib. Med. Angl.* P. 2. pag. 75. *At foſſilia ſive Metallica ſalia alia atq; alia ſunt, & nobis & pene igni dixeram indomabilia.*

not to be maftered, that is, indigeftible
in the Humane Body. Not only therefore
will thefe Caufe, as He very well Argues,
calculous Concretions in the *Kidneys*,
Bladder, and *Joints*; and as *Hippocrates*
experienced, hard Swellings in the *Spleen*;
but they muft necefiarily oftentimes by
their Corrofive quality twitch and irritate the fenfible Membranes of the Stomach and Bowels, and thus hinder and
interrupt the Digeftion of our Food.
Nay, befides all this, when they come
into the Blood, it is no wonder if the
fmall Canals of infenfible Perfpiration
are frequently ftopt and obftructed by
'em; for it is upon this Score that *San-*
ctorius (m) teaches Us, that *heavy Water*
converts the Matter of Tranfpiration into
an Ichor, *which being retained, induces a*
Cachexy.

What Mifchiefs will infue hereupon
every one fees; not only Pains in the
Limbs, livid Spots in the Surface of the
Body, Ulcers, *&c.* from the Acrimony
of the undifcharged Moifture; but many
befides of thofe perplexing Symptoms
which go by the Name of *Hyfterical* and
Hypochondriacal, may take their rife from

(m) *Medicin. Static.* Sect. 2. Aphor. 6.

the

the fame Source ; for the before cited *Sanctorius (n)* has remark'd, that the *Flatus or Wind* fo infeparable from thofe Cafes, is no other than *the Fluid of Perfpiration rude and unfinifhed.*

If thefe Inconveniencies are oftentimes not felt, at leaft not till towards the declining Age, in ftrong and active Habits of Body ; yet I am, from very good Experience, affured, that they deferve Confideration in weaker Conftitutions, and a Sedentary Life, efpecially of the more tender Sex.

I have the honour to be nearly related to a worthy Perfon, who led formerly an afflicted Life from the frequent returns of Violent *Colick Pains*, till fhe was with happy Succefs advifed by the Noble *Van Helmont* not to Drink (as fhe then did) Beer Brewed with *Well-Water* ; and her Health is even now fo far owing to this Management, that an Error in It is unavoidably follow'd with the wonted Complaints.

For thefe Reafons *Pliny (o)* tells Us, that *Thofe Waters are Condemn'd in the firft*

(n) *Ibid.* Sect. 3. Ap. 13. *Flatus nil aliud eft quam rude perfpirabile.*
(o) Lib. 31. c. 3. *Damnantur imprimis Fontes quorum Aquæ decoctæ craffis obducunt Vafa cruftis.*

Place,

Place, which when *Boiled* do *incrustate the sides of the Vessels*; And that our *Well-Waters* do this, no Body who looks into the *Tea-Kettles* of our Gentlewomen can be Ignorant.

And indeed in Ancient Times, when Physick was more a Science, which is now more a Trade, as that Part of It, which relates to *Diet* was more carefully studied, than it is Now-a-days; so this Point particularly of which we are Treating was of so great Moment, that *Hippocrates*, who wrote the best Book *(p)* on the Subject that ever was Publish'd, has in a great Measure accounted not only for the Diseases, but even for the Temper and Disposition of the People of several Countries, from the Difference of the *Waters* with which Nature has supplied Them.

(p) *De Aere, Locis, & Aquis.*

F I N I S.

The Explication of Those Figures which are not Explained in the Treatise.

F*IG*. 1. Reprefents the Head of the *Viper* in its Natural Bignefs, with the Mouth open, and Fangs Erected.

(*a*) Marks the Poifonous *Fang*.
(*b*) The Eye.
(*c*) The Hole of one Noftril.
(*d*) The *Larynx*.
(*e*) The Forked Tongue.

All the Other Figures relating to the Viper *are drawn larger than the Life.*

Fig. 7, & 8. Exhibit fome Mufcles, which ferve for the Motion of the Jaws.

(*a, Fig.*7.) *Elevator Maxillæ Inferioris.*
(*b*) *Depreffor ejufdem.*
(*c*) *Depreffor Dentis Venenofi.*
(*d*) A Strong Ligament faftened by one Extremity to the Spinal *Apophyfis* of the Second *Vertebra* of the Neck, and by the other to the end of the *Elevator Maxillæ Inferioris.*
(*a, Fig.* 8.) A Mufcle, which being fixt to the Extremity of both Jaws, ferves

to

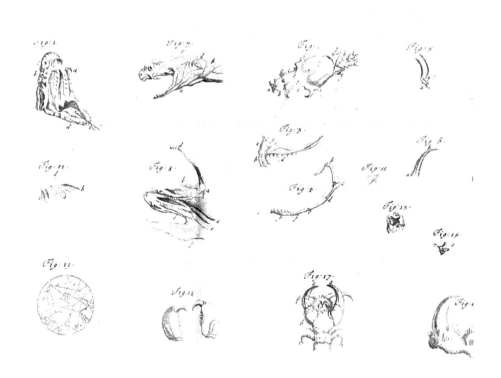

Explication of the Figures.

to pull them backwards, and may be call'd *Retractor*.

(*b*) The Internal fide of the *Depreſſor Dentis Venenoſi.*

(*c*) *Elevator Dentis Venenoſi.*

(*d*) The Extremity of the Lower Jaw.

(*e e*) *Flexores Capitis.*

(*f*) The Internal Part of the Skin covered with ſome Muſcular Fibres.

Fig. 17. Shews the Head of the *Scolopendra.*

(*a a*) The Wounding Claws.

(*b*) The Mouth.

(*c c*) The Two Firſt Feet.

Fig. 18. The Weapons of the *Nhamdu* in their Natural Bigneſs.

CPSIA information can be obtained
at www.ICGtesting.com
Printed in the USA
BVHW081022081118
532529BV00011B/575/P

9 781246 951578